Canada Life Assurance Company

Mortality Experience of the Canada Life Assurance Company

From 1847 to 1893

Canada Life Assurance Company

Mortality Experience of the Canada Life Assurance Company
From 1847 to 1893

ISBN/EAN: 9783337209568

Printed in Europe, USA, Canada, Australia, Japan

Cover: Foto ©ninafisch / pixelio.de

More available books at **www.hansebooks.com**

OF THE

CANADA LIFE

ASSURANCE COMPANY

FROM 1847 TO 1893.

HAMILTON, ONTARIO:
TIMES PRINTING COMPANY.

1893

Canada Life Assurance Company's Offices.

Hamilton, Ont., 1st March, 1895.

A. G. RAMSAY, Esq., F. S. S., F. I. A.,
  Actuary and President,
    Canada Life Assurance Company.

DEAR SIR :

Pursuant to your instructions, and acting under your directions, I have completed the Mortality Investigation so far as at present intended for purpose of publication. With the character and scope of the work you are already familiar, and it is hoped the results brought out will be of interest and service to the Board of Directors and to many others interested in such an investigation.

The work has been done cheerfully, and it is believed carefully, by those to whom you have assigned that duty.

For valuable assistance in the graduation of the Mortality Tables I am indebted to Mr. A. K. Blackadar, M. A., F. I. A., Actuary of the Insurance Department, Ottawa, and to Mr. R. Henderson, B. A., A. I. A., of the same Department.

While this is the first, it is hoped that it will not be the only mortality experience, to be published by a Canadian company, for it is only by such investigations that "facts are substituted for appearances and demonstrations for impressions."

Very respectfully,

FRANK SANDKESON,
  Assistant Actuary.

Mortality Experience

Canada Life Assurance Co'y.

The present investigation into the mortality experience of the Canada Life Assurance Company, from its origin in 1847 to the year 1893—a period of 46 years— possesses more than a local interest.

It is the first investigation of the kind that has been undertaken and published in the Dominion of Canada.

It is, too, the experience of the oldest Canadian Company, a company that has grown up with this young country, and that has become one of its recognized institutions.

It is the experience of a company that has been built up slowly but securely along conservative British lines, and hence it is a better exponent of the rates of mortality in Canada than if its history were shorter, and its volume of business more rapidly and recently secured under the well-known conditions that usually prevail in America. It is, too, the first and only published experience of assured male lives for the northern half of the North American Continent.

Object in View.

Various companies in the United States and elsewhere have published their mortality experience, but the object in view does not in all cases seem to have been the same. In some, every policy on which any premium had been paid was included in the general observations, whether the life was "select," or "rated up," either permanently as an under-average life, or temporarily for occupation or risk of travel

While the resulting rates of mortality may be the actual experience of the company on all its lives, it may not be a very faithful exponent of the mortality prevailing among lives taken as select at the ordinary rate of premium.

The chief object in view in the following investigation has been to determine, for the guidance of the company in particular, and for the benefit of other companies and individuals interested, what rates of mortality have prevailed among male lives which were accepted as "healthy," "select" lives at the usual rate of premium. Then, comparing these rates with those of the Table of Mortality adopted as the official standard, as well as with other Tables, we are enabled to state to what extent the actual experience has deviated from the standard table and from other tables, and whether the contracts now being entered into can, in the distant future, be securely and equitably carried out on the present basis, or whether any change is desirable. Much light is also thrown on the question of selection, and means are afforded for various other subsidiary investigations of importance and interest.

Methods of Treatment.

It follows immediately from the foregoing statement, that all exposures on lives rated-up or charged any extra premium must be rigidly excluded from the general experience. The only exception to this is in the case of lives under 21 years of age, which, according to the practice of the company, are accepted as at 21, but which, in this experience, have been taken at their true age.

The female lives, which were few in number, have also been excluded. As the company has not to any extent dealt in annuities, survivorships or pure endowments, none such are included, so that the present is the experience of assured male lives accepted and continued as "average" lives.

The rated-up male lives (permanent extras) have been dealt with separately. Lives charged a temporary extra for travel, etc., are not included in this experience.

In deciding whether the experience should be developed upon the basis of lives or amounts, the conclusion arrived at was that while an investigation by amounts is of practical interest and of special value when the number of observations is very large, the results by lives would on the whole be preferable where, as in the present case, the number of observations is not large in comparison with several representative and standard experiences. For large experiences an investigation by amounts may be preferred, but for an individual office of moderate size, the results by lives will probably be more regular, and a better guide for the future than those developed by amounts. Lives were therefore adopted as the basis.

For ascertaining the necessary data, the essential particulars of each policy upon which a premium had ever been paid were written on a card of which the following is a copy :

No....... *System*.................... *Amount, $*........

Life...........

If Premium Increased ....

   Occupation...................

Date of	Day, Month, Year.	*Age.*	Duration.
Birth.			
Entry....			
Exit ( )...			

Premium Charged, $..........

Ordinary Premium, $.....

Premium Increased on account of......

Cause of Death..

Remarks..

Although the particulars of "amounts assured," "occupation," and "cause of death" have not been made use of in the present investigation, it was deemed expedient, for future use, to embody these facts on the cards.

Some progress had been made in writing up the particulars on the cards (except the durations and exits) before it was finally decided whether to adopt the well-established calendar year method or the more modern policy year method for tabulating the observations. As this is a point of considerable importance, and as the present experience is intended for the intelligent but non-professional reader as well as for those who are familiar with the principles and methods herein described, it may be well to explain as briefly and as clearly as possible the technical difference between these two methods; under other conditions this and several other of the detailed explanations herein might be omitted.

According to the calendar year method the lives are assumed to enter the company, on the average, at the middle of the calendar year, and (where the office age is the age next birthday, as in British and Canadian companies) the lives are regarded as attaining the office age at the end of the calendar year of entry. Thus the interval between the average date of entry and the attainment of the stated age at entry is assumed to be six months. The first year of assurance is thus seen to contain only six months and is usually called year "0" sometimes also year "1" and sometimes year "$\frac{1}{2}$."

According to the policy year method, calendar years are disregarded, and the risk on each life is traced from anniversary to anniversary of the policy. Thus "year of assurance 1" covers the 12 months following the grant of the assurance; the succeeding 12 months form "year of assurance 2," and so on. By this means we are enabled to allocate each death to the exact policy year in which that death occurred, and hence to determine with precision the true rate of mortality for each policy year of assurance. This is a matter of vital importance, and it constitutes the distinguishing characteristic of the policy year method.

In favor of the adoption of the calendar year method for the present investigation, was the fact that it was much simpler, requiring less data to be extracted, and less time to complete the work. Moreover, this method had been adopted in most of the older and larger published experiences, such as the Combined Experience, the Institute of Actuaries Experience, the 30 American Offices, and the Mutual Life Insurance Co. of New York (1876).

On the other hand, the experiences of the Amicable Society, the Eagle Insurance Co., the Scottish Amicable Society, the Gotha Life (German), and the Connecticut Mutual, have been taken out on the policy year method. In recent years the great superiority of the policy year method, especially in the examination of the effects of selection, has been demonstrated.

After a careful examination into all the advantages of each method, it was decided to adopt the policy year method.

The office age at entry, i. e., age next birthday, was from the first entered upon the cards, partly by reason of the above uncertainty of the adoption of the calendar or policy year method, and partly because in some of the older assurances the date of birth was not obtainable.

Under other circumstances the mean age, or the nearest age at entry, would doubtless have been adopted, and this would have avoided the reduction of the experience from odd to even ages, as explained later on.

An examination of various published mortality experiences has led to the conviction that in some cases a great deal of their value has been lessened by the absence of detailed explanations and facts which are necessary in attempting to assign the true weight to any particular features.

It has been thought desirable, therefore, on the present occasion, to state explicitly the various steps and principles involved, so that when any comparisons or investigations are instituted, the underlying circumstances may be known.

Classification and Reduction of the Data.

The principal particulars having been entered from the office registers on the cards, these were then all carefully checked over. All permanent and temporary rated-up lives, as well as all female lives, were then eliminated from the general experience. For the reasons previously indicated the age at entry was the office age, i. e., age next birthday. The next step was to fill in the mode of exit, and it was decided to tabulate the "exits" under the four subdivisions : Existing, Matured, Withdrawn and Died. The matured contain expired term assurances and matured endowment assurances, and the withdrawn compose lapsed and surrendered cases. It is true the matured constitute but a small portion of the whole, but in view of the uncertainty created by the inclusion of these as an unknown factor among the withdrawals when the rate of discontinuance is under discussion, it was thought advisable to make a separate class of them. It is not to be understood, however, that all the matured endowment assurance policies of the company appear under the head of "matured," for, as frequently happens, if a life were still existing under a life policy, and an endowment assurance (upon which the risk was continuous with the life policy) had matured prior to the close of the observations, the endowment assurance card would have been combined with the life card, and the life assured thereunder would be classed under the head of "existing." The "exits" were all checked with the office registers.

The term policies have been so limited in number, and have apparently exercised so little, if any, adverse influence on the mortality of the company, that it was not thought necessary to exclude them, which latter course, under other circumstances, would have been desirable. It is hoped that the separation of the matured from the withdrawn, and the publication of the data of these two classes in detail (an unusual course for an individual company) will be of service to any persons who may wish to make further use of this experience in examining the rate of discontinuance.

With regard to the important question of the duration of the risks, the existing were carried to the anniversaries of the policies in the year 1893, the duration being found by subtracting the year of entry from the year 1893, thus giving an integral number of years in all existing cases. The deaths have been carefully located in the policy year in which death took place, this being an essential feature of the policy year method. The original observations being scheduled by years of assurance and not by ages at exit, the "deaths" were, as is usual, observed to the close of the year, thus giving the duration as an integer in each case. The age at death in the aggregate table of mortality is the age at entry plus the *curtate* duration.

For the withdrawn and the matured the "nearest duration method" was adopted.

When the duration was, say, $n + \frac{1}{2}$ years, the $\frac{1}{2}$ was alternately dropped and increased $\frac{1}{2}$. In the first year of assurance the duration of a withdrawal at the end of three months was taken as "0"; at the end of nine months as "1" year, and at the end of six months alternately as "0" and "1". A corresponding course was pursued in succeeding years of assurance.

It being decided to develop the experience upon lives, the next step was to bring together all cards relating to the same life.

The presence of the date of birth on most of the cards greatly facilitated the examination into cases where both Christian name and surname were the same. After the cards had thus been brought together a number of cases were discovered in which discrepancies as to age existed by reason of the assured having given different dates of birth in different applications. In such cases (if the life were still assured) circular letters were sent out asking for evidence as to the correct date. By this means a number of the discrepancies were rectified. If the life passed out of observation by death, the age at entry was adjusted by means of the date of birth given in the claim papers. When no information was obtainable, as on lives withdrawn, it usually happened that from the examination of the cards the dates on two or three or four cards would be the same and that on one card different. In such cases the prevailing date was adopted for determining the age at entry. In all other cases the date of birth given on the first application was adopted, where obtainable.

The next step was to examine whether or not the assurances on the same life were continuous. Where the risk on different policies was continuous the cards were placed in an envelope, with the proper duration and other particulars from the cards placed on the back, and these policies were afterwards treated as one continuous risk on one life. Thus the observations were reduced from policies to lives. From this point, therefore, we deal only with *lives*.

In the next place, the cards, thus reduced, were sorted into Existing, Withdrawn, Matured and Died. Each of these groups was then sorted according to age at entry (next birthday). Each of these sub-groups was then further sub-divided according to years of assurance. The cards in each of these final sub-groups were then counted and tabulated in the form in which they are now published. After the cards had been thus counted and scheduled, the next step was the calculation of the "Exposed to Risk of Death." To illustrate this take age at entry 25 (Table I). There are 1765 entrants, of whom 67 withdrew within six months, that is, these 67 are composed of all the withdrawals at the end of the first quarter, and one-half the withdrawals at the end of the second quarter. As before explained, these are held not to have been under observation, but are simply recorded and used when dealing with the rate of discontinuance. The remaining 1698 are, as a consequence of the "nearest duration method," held to have been at risk throughout the whole year. At the end of "year 1" 362 pass out of observation—6 by death, 278 as withdrawn, and 78 as existing—leaving 1336 exposed to risk during "year of assurance 2," of whom 151 pass from observation at the end of the year—9 by death, 88 withdrawn and 54 existing.

The "exposed to risk" for the remaining years of assurance are similarly calculated.

Range of the Experience.

As indicated at the outset, the present experience covers a period of 46 years, and the years of life exposed were 296,481. Hence, while the number of observations is not so great relatively as in several other experiences, the period over which the observations extend is such as to make the results of special value. The total number of entrants was 35,287, of whom 55.03 per cent. were existing at the close of the observations in 1893; 37.07 per cent had withdrawn and matured; and 7.9 per cent had died.

The average age at entry (next birthday) was 32.05 and the average duration of membership was 8.40 years, or 8.36 years counting the year of death as one-half year. As a matter of caution to some persons who frequently draw wrong conclusions from such figures, it may be stated that the average duration of membership of those who died was 13.55 years, counting the year of death as a whole year. In the following table these averages are brought into comparison with those of three large representative experiences.

	Average duration of one Died. Years.	Average duration of the Total Entrants. Years.
20 British Offices (Hm)	13.50	9.22
30 American Offices	5.94	4.40
23 German Offices	9.81	6.52
Canada Life	13.55	8.40

The average duration of the died in the Canada Life was almost identical with that in the Hm. experience, and more than twice as great as in the 30 American Offices.

Among individual offices the average duration of membership was as follows : Mutual Life, N. Y., 5.67 years; Mutual Benefit, N. J., 6.53 years; Connecticut Mutual, 7.98 years ; Australian Mutual Provident Society, 6.20 years.

In the following table is given a summary of the data contained in the present investigation.

Existing.		Withdrawn and Matured.		Died.		Total Entrants.	Total Years of Life.	Av. duration of Membership. Years.	Average Age at Entry.	
Number	Percent of Entrants	Number	Percent of Entrants	Number	Percent of Entrants				Age attained.	Age next Birthday.
19,419	55.03	13,079	37.07	2,789	7.90	35,287	296,481	8.40	31.72	32.05

As will be seen when dealing with the rate of discontinuance, nearly half the withdrawals belong to the first year of assurance.

As a matter of record and to aid in forming some idea of the different circumstances and characteristics of mortality experiences frequently referred to, it may be well to bring together, as in the following table, the principal features of each.

TABLE SHOWING THE DATA OF DIFFERENT MORTALITY EXPERIENCES.

In the Amicable, Scottish Amicable, Gotha Life, Connecticut Mutual and Canada Life Experience the Policy Year Method was used, in the others the Calendar Year Method.

The original facts used in the construction of the various tables will be found in Table I., extending from age 15 at entry to 71. **Table II.** is a summary of the observations in Table I.

To assist in referring from the tables to their explanation herein, the number of the table is printed in black-faced type where first referred to.

The Mortality Table.

Having briefly explained the preliminary steps that led up to the tabulation of the data as in Table I., it is now necessary to state how the final aggregate table of mortality has been deduced.

The data in Table I. was first scheduled according to "exposed" and "died" for each age attained (next birthday). As previously stated, the age attained for the "died" is the age at entry plus the curtate duration of the "died". Up to this point the ages are those for next birthday, and it now became necessary to deal, as is customary, with completed ages.

During the progress of the investigation the cards had been sampled and it was found by various trials that the office age or age next birthday was, on an average, approximately one-third of a year greater than the true age at entry, and it was determined to use this fraction of a year in place of the usual half year in reducing the experience from fractional to integral ages. The original facts used in the construction of the general table, viz.: the exposures and deaths at ages $14\frac{2}{3}$, $15\frac{2}{3}$, etc., will be found in **Table III., Part I.,** the argument being set down one-third greater than the real age. From these the values of log $p_{x-\frac{1}{3}}$ were taken out, and then by continuous addition those of log $l_{x-\frac{1}{3}}$ were obtained. The values of $l_{x-\frac{1}{3}}$ were then taken out, and by differencing those of $d_{x-\frac{1}{3}}$ were derived; and the values of l_x were deduced from the formula $l_x = l_{x-\frac{1}{3}} - \frac{1}{3}d_{x-\frac{1}{3}}$. In consequence of the paucity of the data under age 20, the table begins at age 20 with a radix of 10,000. Thus was obtained **Table III., Part 2.**

This table is the starting point for a graduation by Woolhouse's or Higham's formula, each of which was tried. The latter was the more satisfactory, but as the values of q_x were slightly irregular at the extremities of the table, it was finally decided to adopt a graduation by Makeham's formula, using the method of Messrs. King and Hardy (slightly modified) to determine the constants. The modification consisted in using the values of log l_x in place of those of log l_x, with the consequent changes in the formula for determining the constants. This was done to avoid the assumption contained in the formula $l_x = l_{x-1} - \frac{1}{2} d_{x-1}$.

The particular combination of ages finally selected for determining the constants, was four periods of fifteen years, from ages $20\frac{3}{4}$ to $79\frac{3}{4}$ inclusive. The usual constants, s, g and c, of Makeham's formula were first determined so that $\Delta \Sigma_{n}^{m} \log l_{x+n}$, $\Delta \Sigma_{n}^{m} l_x$, $\Delta \Sigma_{n}^{m} l_x$, should be the same in the adjusted and unadjusted tables.

Having found the values of s, g and c, the value of k is then determined from $\log k = 5 - 20 \log s - c^{20} \log g$. thus starting the graduated table at age 20, with a radix of 100,000.

The values of the constants thus formed are as follows :

$$\log c = .04253477 \qquad \log s = \overline{1}.998145123$$
$$\log g = \overline{1}.999781412 \qquad \log k = 5.03566480$$

The values of $\log(-\Delta \log p_x)$, $-\Delta \log p_x$, $\log p_x$, $\log l_x$, l_x and q_x were then successfully derived, q_x being formed from $\log p_x$. The complete expectation of life for each age was then calculated. The mortality table thus graduated will be found in Table IV.

To test how closely the expected deaths agreed with the actual deaths by the graduated table, it was necessary to devise some means of bringing the original exposures and deaths to integral ages. The method adopted was to put in the column of exposed opposite age x, $2 E_{x-\frac{1}{2}} + E_{x+\frac{1}{2}}$, and in the column of deaths $2d_{x-\frac{1}{2}} + d_{x+\frac{1}{2}}$, when E is the exposed and d the deaths, thus showing the exposures and deaths at three times their real number.

The number of expected deaths was then calculated by multiplying $2 E_{x-\frac{1}{2}} + E_{x+\frac{1}{2}}$ by q_x. Theoretically it will be found that the column of expected deaths is thus made very slightly greater than its true value.

On the above basis of three times the original exposures, the total expected deaths was practically equal to the number of actual deaths. As the original table of three times the exposures and deaths for integral ages (above referred to) is used later on as the basis of other tables, it is given in Table V., beginning with age 19.

Before proceeding to make any observations on the rates of mortality, as shown in the foregoing tables, the method of constructing the select tables will first be taken up.

The Select Mortality Tables.

The superiority of the policy year method over the calendar method in examining the gradual wearing out of the benefits of selection in the early years of assurance is now an established fact. Hence it seemed desirable on the present occasion, notwithstanding the comparative smallness of the data, to show, at least approximately, this effect of selection.

In the work of forming select tables from the observations, the first step was to construct a table omitting the first five years of assurance. There being no observations above age 73 during these first five years, and very few for the ages (during the same period) immediately preceding 73, the rates of mortality from 73 and upwards would be the same as in the general table, and these latter have accordingly been adopted for the experience after five years.

By means of the graphic method a table was constructed representing the experience after five years and joining on smoothly to the general experience at age 73. This table was tested by comparing actual with expected deaths, and when a serious discrepancy occurred the curve was amended and re-tested until a satisfactory series was obtained.

The original facts and the final adjusted rates of mortality after five years will be found in **Table VI.**

Having thus obtained a table representing the mortality among lives assured more than five years, it is required, in order to complete the select tables, to determine the mortality during the first five years for each age at entry.

In consequence of the paucity of materials below age 20 and over age 50, the select tables for these years are limited to ages 20 to 50.

For the first year of assurance the exposures and deaths were combined into three groups. The actual and expected death rates in each group were then calculated and the actual death rate set down opposite the age corresponding to the expected. A series proceeding by constant second differences was then determined to pass through these values. The ages and rates were: Age $27\frac{3}{4}$, rate .00265; age $37\frac{1}{4}$, rate .00355; age $46\frac{3}{4}$, rate .00506, from which we get $q_{\text{[x]}} = .0023695\text{S}$, Δ .00001326 and $\Delta' = .05000679$. The calculations were facilitated by the intervals of age coming out equal.

To determine the rates of mortality in the third year of assurance the exposures and deaths in the second, third and fourth years of assurance for each present age were combined, and from the rates of mortality thus calculated a hypothetical unadjusted mortality table was constructed, which was then graduated by Makeham's formula assuming the value of c the same as in the general table. The rates of mortality calculated from this table were taken as the rates of mortality in the third year of of assurance.

For the second, fourth and fifth years of assurance the rates of mortality were determined independently by interpolation with constant fourth differences.

Thus have been found the rates of mortality in the first, second, third, fourth and fifth years of assurance respectively, and also those after five years of assurance. These rates are given in **Table VII.** Although deduced from limited data, yet the graduated results show a general consistency with the original facts.

From an examination of the mortality of the first year of assurance, it will be seen that the rates are remarkably low, and it might be inferred that some influence such as the dating back of policies had brought about this result by the introduction of a period of exposure where no risk was incurred, but it must be remembered that among the lapses (which are most numerous during the first year of assurance), there is a period of 30 days grace not included in the exposures, and this may be taken as an offset to any non-risk period at the inception of the policy.

A word of explanation to the general reader may be necessary as to the notation used in Table VII. The symbol $q_{[20]}$, for example, denotes the probability that a life aged 20, which has just been accepted as a "select" or healthy life, will die within one year; $q_{[20]+1}$ is the probability that the same life (should it live through the first year) will die in the second year of assurance; $q_{[20]+2}$ is the probability that the same life (if still assured at the end of second year) will die in the third year, and so on; $q_{x(5)}$ denotes the rate of mortality, or probability of dying in a year, of a life that has been assured 5 years and is now aged x. The column $q_{x(5)}$ therefore gives the rates of mortality, excluding the first five years of assurance.

From the rates of mortality in Table VII., the values of l, were determined so that in that part of the table in which the rate of mortality was the same as in the general graduated table, the numbers in the column of living should also be the same.

These values are brought together in **Table VIII.**, the notation used having a corresponding meaning to that already given to Table VII.

Having obtained the values of l_x and q_x, excluding the first five years of assurance, from age 25 upwards, it will be convenient to have these and relative functions brought together in the form of a graduated mortality table similar to the graduated Table IV for the whole experience.

This has been done in **Table IX**. As before explained, the values of l_x, d_x, q_x and e are the same in both from age 74 upwards.

Table X gives the graduated experience of the Canada Life, Mutual Life and H^m, excluding the first five years of assurance. It must be remembered, however, that in consequence of the calendar year process only $4\frac{1}{2}$ years are really excluded in the case of the H^m and Mutual Life experiences, the rates being therefore those derived from the experience after $4\frac{1}{2}$ years. Whatever difference is thus created will be in favor of the two experiences just named.

The results given in Tables VII. and VIII. above make it possible to construct tables of annuities, premiums and reserves for lives recently selected, and thus to measure the effect which the benefits of selection have upon the financial operations of a life assurance company. This is foreign to the present investigation, but the subject is of great importance in its bearing upon the ultimately successful conduct of any company.

Observations and Comparisons.

A cursory examination of the graduated mortality table of the Canada Life Assurance Co., both for the whole duration as well as for the period excluding the first five years of assurance, will at once make it evident that the experience of the Company has been remarkably favorable. This is more remarkable when it is said that the volume of new business transacted yearly has not been large when compared with many companies in America; and further, that the whole life assurance business has always been much larger than the endowment assurance business, on the former of which the death loss is generally believed to be heavier than on the latter.

Although neither the system nor the amounts of assurance enter into separate investigation on the present occasion, it may be well to state the relation between the sums assured on life, endowment and other assurances. This is done in the following table, which embraces the whole business of the company, and from which it will be seen that at the end of 1889 the endowment assurances were less than 16% of the whole life assurances, and at the end of 1893 they were $17\frac{1}{4}$% of the latter, thus showing an increased percentage of endowment assurances, but the relative amount of such assurances is not large when compared with that in many other companies in America

	Whole Life Assurances.	Endowment Assurances.	All other Assurances.	Bonus Additions.	Total Assurances in Force.
31st Dec., 1889...	$40,919,588	$6,435,509	$106,545	$2,058,417	$49,519,559
31st Dec., 1893...	51,027,429	8,807,016	90,545	2,783,256	62,703,246

In view of future comparisons it is well, therefore, to keep in mind (1) that the volume of business has been of continuous, but not rapid growth ; (2) that whole life assurances largely predominate ; (3) that only male lives accepted and continued as "average" lives are included in the present general experience.

To bring into clear view the results of the tables of mortality already described, a series of tables of comparison has been compiled, to which attention is now drawn. By means of these it will be possible to measure to some extent the satisfactory character of the present experience. At the same time, the characteristics and surroundings of each experience must be kept steadily in view, so that undue weight may not be attached to the conclusions which appear to follow from the comparisons.

Expectation of Life.

The first table of comparison is that showing the expectation of life, or average after-life time, according to various graduated tables of mortality. For the United States the expectation of life by four tables are brought into view, viz. : the American Experience, the 30 American Offices, the Mutual Life of New York, and the Mutual Benefit of New Jersey ; for Great Britain three tables—the Institute of Actuaries (H^m), the Equitable, and the Law Life ; for Germany one table—the Gotha Life ; for Australia one table—the Australian Mutual Provident Society. To the interesting mortality experience of the last named company, published in 1888, an acknowledgment is due on the present occasion for some figures relating to two or three experiences not easily obtainable.

The expectation of life by these various tables and by the Canada Life experience will be found in Table XI.

Omitting for a moment the Australian Mutual Provident experience, it will be seen from Table XI. that the expectation of life by the Canada Life experience exceeds at all ages that of all the other experiences. It will also be seen that the Mutual Life results at the insuring ages run quite close to, but below those of the Canada Life.

The Standard tables, embracing the experiences of various companies, show a considerably lower expectation throughout than the Canada Life.

For the Australian Mutual Provident Society two columns are given, one according to assumed ages and one according to true ages. The expectations of life by the former exceed those of the Canada Life, while those by the latter are less. It is not possible, therefore, from this table to say which is the more favorable. Further investigation will, it is believed, show that the Canada Life experience is quite as favorable as that of the Australian Mutual Provident, if not more so, when the differing circumstances are taken into account.

Other Comparisons.

For the benefit of many persons, especially in Canada, who have not in their possession the rates of mortality of well-known mortality experiences, Table XII. is given, showing the graduated annual rates of mortality at each age according to the experiences of the Canada Life, American Experience, 30 American Offices, Institute of Actuaries (H^m), Mutual Life of New York, and Mutual Benefit of New Jersey. In the same table will be found the ratio of the Canada Life mortality at each age to that of the other tables mentioned.

From this table it will be seen that the Canada Life mortality is less at all ages than that of the tables named, except from ages 51 to 65 of the Mutual Life of New York, where it is slightly greater. A comparison of this table will show that neither the American experience table nor the Institute of Actuaries (H^m) experience is a very faithful exponent of the mortality as experienced by the Canada Life, the first-named experience, especially, showing, for the younger ages, rates considerably in excess of those of the Canada Life. It must be remembered, however, that the rates at the younger ages in the present experience are those produced very largely by recent selection, and are, therefore, no doubt lower than would ultimately prevail.

The 30 American Offices experience would seem to run more nearly parallel with that of the Canada Life than either of the other two just mentioned. As between the Mutual Life and Mutual Benefit, the latter experience runs more evenly at all ages with that of the Canada Life than the former.

The experiences of these two companies (Mutual Life and Mutual Benefit) were doubtless not confined as exclusively to "average" male lives as the present experience, which would tend to make the latter appear more favorable, but on the other hand, in deducing the rates of these two companies no adjustment appears to have been made for reducing the experience from fractional to integral ages, as was done in the case of the 30 American Offices' experience. Had this adjustment been made, the experience of the Canada Life would have appeared in comparison still more favorable, especially at the older ages. In the case of the Mutual Life the favorable deviation between ages 51 and 65 previously referred to would have thus practically disappeared.

To make still more clear the difference between the mortality experienced by the Canada Life and other companies, **Table XIII.** is given, showing the exposures and deaths (unadjusted) by quinquennial groups of ages and the expected deaths by other experiences. The exposures for integral ages attained are derived from Table V. by taking one-third thereof, the deaths being taken to the nearest whole number.

From this table it will be seen that from age 20 to 79 the total actual and expected deaths, and the percentages of the one to the other, are as follows :

Actual Deaths Canada Life	Mutual Life	Mutual Benefit	Connecticut Mutual (Males)	American Experience Table	Thirty American Offices	H.M. Table	British Amicable Fund	Alpha Life	American Mutual Premiums 1868	
									At Assumed Ages	At Time Ages
2748	2973.6	3224.3	3136.2	3726.1	3400.3	3853.2	3261	3768.2	2621.6	2899.9
Percentages to above	92.4	85	87.6	73.8	80.4	71.2	89.3	74.1	104.8	93.1

This extract from Table XIII. will at once illustrate the very satisfactory character of the mortality experienced by the Canada Life Assurance Company.

Table XIV. gives the rates of mortality per cent. for quinquennial groups of ages as deduced from each experience therein mentioned. In the case of the American Experience the rates are deduced from the graduated table.

The Influence of Selection.

The next group of tables deals with the effects of selection by different experiences. Graduated select tables for the present experience have already been referred to and given in **Tables VII. and VIII.** The tables now to be discussed deal with ungraduated results.

In **Table XV.** the exposures and deaths for all ages combined are arranged according to years of assurance. As the data after 30 years' duration is small in most of the experiences, the comparison is therefore confined to the first thirty years of assurance. In making this comparison caution must be exercised in view of the different characteristics of the experiences. Thus the average age at entry is greater in some than in others. In the case of the II^m table this will partly explain the large excess of expected deaths. Again, the Connecticut Mutual and the Canada Life are the only experiences taken out on the policy year method, the others being on the calendar year plan, with only six months for year of assurance 1. In place of attempting the unsatisfactory task of harmonizing calendar and policy year experiences, the first six months of the calendar year experiences has been treated as "year 1," the annual rate for the usual "year 0" being taken as the rate for the complete year. Whatever difference is thus created will be in favor of the other experiences and adverse to those of the Canada Life and Connecticut Mutual.

In examining Tables XV., XVI. and XVII. the following facts must be kept steadily in view

Average	Canada Life.	Mutual Life.	Connecticut Mutual.	Mutual Benefit	II^m	30 American Offices.	A. M. P. Society.
Age at entry..............	31.72	34.95			34.96	35.23	32.
Duration of membership...	8.40	5.67	7.98	6.53	9.22	4.40	6.20

It will be seen that the average age at entry in the Canada Life agrees more nearly with that given for the A. M. P. Society than with that in any of the others. But the average age at entry for the 71,542 healthy lives in the above society was 31 years, while the average true age at entry for the 38,757 rated up lives was 30.22 years. Thus it will be apparent the average *true* age at entry in the above society was less than in the Canada Life.

After making allowance for different characteristics as shown in the foregoing table, it will still be apparent from Table XVII. that the benefits of selection have been very marked in the present experience.

Table XVII. shows the ratios per cent. (by years of assurance) of the actual deaths in the Canada Life to the expected deaths by the other experiences mentioned. In the last three or four years of some of the experiences the rates are based on limited data, so that some unevenness is to be expected in the results for those years.

In the three previous tables the ages are all combined, and the weight of observation at different ages at exposure is ignored. Hence, to form a more reliable comparison, the experience is divided in **Table XVIII.** according to ages at exposure, **Part 1** giving the experience during the first five years and **Part 2** the experience after five years. To obtain the exposures in groups for integral ages attained, two-thirds of the exposures for the first age in the original group are thrown off, and one-third of the exposures for the first age (next birthday) in the next group are added on; and similarly for the deaths—thus reducing the experience from fractional to integral ages attained. For the experiences other than the Canada Life and the Connecticut Mutual the rates of mortality for the first five years are really based on only four and one-half years' experience, in accordance with the calendar year method. The comparisons in Tables XVIII. and XIX. are, therefore, in this respect in favor of the experiences based on calendar years.

From Table XVII. it will be seen that the experience of the A. M. P. Society approaches more nearly to that of the Canada Life than any of the others. During the first thirty years the total deaths in the Canada Life (all ages combined) are 97.6% of the expected deaths in the A. M. P. Society. In Table XVIII. it will be seen that for the first five years of assurance there is very little difference in the two experiences, even when taking the A. M. P. experience at the assumed ages, so that no real superiority for Australian lives is here shown. The Scottish Widows' Fund and Canada Life experiences during the first five years are practically identical, the actual and expected deaths being 680 and 684 respectively.

From the comparatively large number of exposures on recently selected lives it might be inferred that the favorable character of the present experience (as shown by the aggregate or mixed table of mortality in which assurances of all durations are combined) would not hold true when comparisons are made in which the first five years of assurance are excluded. The proportion of total exposures belonging to the first five years of assurance was 43% in the Canada Life and 48 in the Connecticut Mutual, while the proportion of total exposures belonging to the first 4½ calendar years was 55 in the Mutual Life, 49% in the A. M. P. experience, 41, in the Mutual Benefit, 39% in the 11ᵐ and 32 in the Scottish Widows' Fund. In the 30 American Offices the proportion was 65%.

Table XVIII., Part 2, shows that the actual deaths after five years' duration in the Canada Life are less than the expected deaths by the Mutual Benefit, Connecticut

Mutual, Mutual Life, Scottish Widows' Fund and H^m experiences, a fact which establishes the superior quality of assured lives in Canada.

There is a very marked regularity between the Mutual Benefit and Canada Life mortality after five years for each group of ages, the former being almost throughout slightly in excess of the latter, and on the whole nearly 5°/. in excess ; but it should be noted that the Mutual Benefit experience is of shorter duration than that of the Canada Life.

In the experience after five years it must be remembered that as between the Canada Life and A. M. P. experiences the longer durations of the risks in the former and the rating up of the lives in the latter are disturbing factors, both in favor of the A. M. P. Society. The practice of rating up the lives in the latter company (35°/. of the lives being rated up) had the effect of making the mortality appear about 10°', more favorable than if all the lives had been accepted at their true ages. Moreover, the large endowment assurance business had the effect of reducing the deaths by about 3°/.. When Table XVIII. is read in the light of these facts it cannot be said that the experience of assured lives in Australia is more favorable than in Canada.

An examination of the foregoing tables will show that the experience of the Canada Life Assurance Company has been quite as favorable as that of any of the other experiences examined, if not more so.

The Mortuary Statistics of Canada, as published in the Dominion Census of 1891, show a very low death rate when compared with similar statistics of other countries. Assuming the substantial accuracy of the Census, we have here evidence that confirms the experience of the Canada Life, that Canada is one of the healthiest countries in the world. With a lower rate of mortality and a higher rate of interest than prevails in most countries, a well managed Canadian company, therefore, possesses special advantages in its claims to public patronage.

Table XIX gives the rates of mortality for the first five years, and after five years, for the experiences mentioned.

It is generally supposed that the benefits of selection are worn out by the end of the fifth year. To ascertain how far this is true in the present experience the rates of mortality, excluding the first five years of assurance, were compared with those excluding the first ten years of assurance, and it was found that after age 34 the rates for quinquennial groups of ages were practically the same in both.

As a further contribution to the study of the effects of selection, **Table XX**. is given in summary form only. **Part 1** shows the rates by quinquennial years of assurance and central ages at entry ; age 20, for example, being the (approximate) centre for the five ages at entry 18 to 22, the exposures and deaths being reduced to integral ages before deducing the rates of mortality. The rapid rise in the rates of mortality as the life grows older and further away from the point of selection is strikingly shown in this table (Part I). For example, taking age 40 at entry, the rate for the first five years is only 5.08 per thousand. For the third five years (11 to 15) the rate is more than doubled, being 11 57 per thousand, while for the fifth five years (21 to 25) the rate is more than five times what it was the first five years, being 28.88 per thousand ; and after 30 years' duration the original rate, 5.08, has increased to 62 77 per thousand, or more than twelve times the rate for the first five years.

To wilfully ignore these facts and to mislead innocent persons by disregarding their ultimate effects, is to commit a crime against society.

Part 2 of **Table XX**. shows the rates by quinquennial years of assurance and quinquennial groups of ages (next birthday) at exposure.

This table confirms the investigations of Messrs. Sprague, King and others, viz. : that shortly after entry the lives, on the average, seriously deteriorate, but afterwards show a marked improvement. Thus, examining the rates in the above-named table it will be seen that while there is a sudden rise in the rates for the second five years, an improvement is usually shown either in the third or fourth quinquennium.

The most natural explanation of this is that the large number of healthy lives withdrawing in the early years brings about a deterioration in the body of remaining lives, thus causing the higher resulting rate in the second five years, but after the effect of this has worn off an improvement takes place. It follows from this that if a company were to guarantee from the outset the full reserve each year as a surrender value, thus offering a temptation for healthy lives to withdraw, a serious injustice might result to the persistent members.

From the mortality table (IX), excluding the first five years of assurance, the commutation columns D, and N, have been calculated, using 4% as the rate of interest. From these the values of the life annuities, a, , are at once obtained. These values will be found in **Table XXI**.

Experience on Rated=up Lives.

As previously stated. all rated-up lives were carefully eliminated from the general experience. The rated-up cases were divided into two classes, viz. : permanent extras and temporary extras, the latter including cases where a loading or fine was imposed to cover some temporary or special risk. These latter have not been included in this investigation, but the experience of the permanently rated-up lives has been separately dealt with

Table XXII. gives the result of this investigation. The number of entrants dealt with was 734, of whom 89 died. The average loading was approximately 3¼ years. The experience was first developed according to actual ages, and afterwards according to assumed ages, and the exposed and died then grouped by quinquennial ages at exposure. Comparison was then made with the expected number of deaths according to the company's general experience (original), and also with the H^m experience.

It was found that while the number of actual deaths at actual ages was 89, the expected number by the company's general experience was only 75, while the expected number by the H^m table was 106. On the other hand, while the number of deaths at assumed ages was, as before, 89, the expected number by the company's general experience was 86, and by the H^m table 120.

From this it follows that the management of the Company have practically succeeded in the difficult task of putting the rated-up lives on an equality with the "average" lives. It will be seen also that the actual number of deaths was well within the expected number by the H^m table, even at true ages.

The smallness of the data renders further investigation into this class of doubtful practical value.

On the Rate of Discontinuance.

When the present investigation was commenced the question of an enquiry into the rates of discontinuance was regarded as of secondary importance, but as the work progressed it was felt that the practical bearing of this question on the finance of life assurance, and the opportunity for its elucidation by means of the data now at hand, demanded that some attention should be given to this subject.

In obtaining the rates of mortality by years of assurance, we have seen that it is a necessary condition of the policy year method that the deaths should be allocated to the policy year in which death takes place.

If it were thought necessary to obtain with equal precision the rate of discontinuance, it would have been necessary to tabulate the discontinuances in a manner similar to the deaths, i. e., in the exact policy year of discontinuance. But in view of the fact that the rate of discontinuance is less regular than that of mortality, differing according to different companies, different plans of assurance and other circumstances, it was thought that for the present purpose, at least, the tabulation of the withdrawals, according to the nearest duration method, would give results sufficiently approximate for all practical purposes.

From the explanation given on page 10 it will be remembered that the withdrawals are made to pass from observation at the end of the policy year. In consequence of this the rate of discontinuance is determined as at the end of the year, and not in the year. The function tabulated, therefore, is not exactly the same as in some other experiences. In obtaining the exposed to risk of discontinuance the deaths have been deducted from the exposed to risk of death, thus giving the exposed to risk of discontinuance at the end of the year. For example : in "year of assurance 1" there were 34,046 exposed to risk of death (all ages combined) and 112 deaths. Subtracting these deaths, we get 33,934 exposed to risk of discontinuance, and it is found that 4,836 withdrew at the end of year 1. The percentage of discontinuance is, therefore, 14.25. This is, therefore, the proportion of lives that do not pass on to the second year. Similarly with succeeding years. These particulars will be found in Table XXIII.

The nearest duration method makes it difficult to deal satisfactorily with the first year of assurance, as there are a number who pass from observation at the end of the first and second quarters, the majority being at the end of six months.

In addition to the discontinuances at the end of year 1, we have therefore to deal also with these quarterly cases, which, as explained on page 10, are composed of all the withdrawals at the end of the first quarter and one-half of those at the end of the second quarter.

In the absence of any more approved method these have been placed under "year 0" and the exposed taken as the total number of entrants.

In grouping any number of years of assurance together to obtain an average annual ratio of discontinuances, the exposures under year 0 have been divided by 2.

Table XXIII. gives the exposed and discontinued by years of assurance for all ages combined, and the per cent discontinued ; also the expected discontinuances by the experience of the Connecticut Mutual on premium-paying life policies. The discontinuances were treated similarly in these two experiences, except that the compulsory withdrawals (matured term and endowment assurances) were separately dealt with in the Canada Life investigation, but in the comparison in Table XXIII, the percentages for the Connecticut Mutual are those based on life policies, so that no matured term or endowment assurances enter into the question. An examination of this table will show that the discontinuances are considerably lower in the Canada Life than on the above mentioned section of the Connecticut Mutual experience.

To form some relative idea of the rates of discontinuance in other experiences Table XXIV. is given, showing the rates by the Mutual Life, Australian Mutual Provident, 30 American Offices, H^m Table and 23 German Offices, the rates for the last two being extracted from Mr. McClintock's essay, "On the Effects of Selection," except that for year o in the H^m, the annual rate 2.7 has been supplied from other sources.

The function tabulated in this table is not quite the same as in Table XXIII. Moreover, the rate tabulated by the Mutual Life of New York is based on the exposed to risk of death, while in the others one-half the deaths are properly deducted from the exposed to risk of death before deducing the rate. But the actual change in the rates by reason of these differences is probably too small to invalidate any general conclusions drawn from a comparison of the figures in these two tables.

The comparatively large number of discontinuances in and at the end of the first year in the Canada Life Assurance Company seems to a considerable extent due to the practice of writing policies quarterly and half-yearly when requested. Besides, the period of severe competition for new business is included in the present experience and this will have considerable weight on the first year's withdrawals.

After year 2 the experience follows very closely that of the H^m table. In the early years of assurance of the A. M. P. Society the rate of discontinuance is favorably influenced by the non-forfeiture conditions of that company's policies, but after the eighth year the Canada Life shows a considerably lower percentage of discontinuances. Allowance has to be made, however, for the effect of matured endowment assurances in the later years of assurance in the case of the A. M. P. Society.

From years 2 to 8, inclusive, the discontinuance experiences of the Canada Life and Mutual Life are very similar, but from year 9 onwards the proportion is considerably less in the case of the Canada Life; while throughout the first fifteen years it is much more favourable than that of the 30 American Offices. On the whole, therefore, it may be said that the Canada Life Assurance Co. shows a very favourable experience as regards discontinuances.

It is sometimes maintained that the rate of discontinuance is sufficiently regular in different companies to give effect to its influence in calculating premium rates. While it is not impossible to take into account the discontinuance rate as well as the death rate in calculating premiums, yet in view of the varied circumstances that go to influence the withdrawals, it would be necessary to use such a conservative estimate for future discontinuances that it is very doubtful if the consequent reduction in premiums would compensate the assured for the loss of privileges enjoyed under the present system.

In view of the many fallacious arguments used in Canada and the United States as to the rate of discontinuance and the effect thereof, it may be well to emphasize the fact that out of 12,891 discontinuances in 46 years of the Canada Life experience 6,077 withdrew within one year (or at most within one year and a half) from entry.

Now, when the cost of procuring these assurances is considered—the medical fee, the agent's commission, issue of policy, and the proportionate amount of other general expenses, together with the cost of carrying the risk—it cannot truthfully be said that a company makes large gains from these lapses.

Omitting, therefore, the lapses of "year 1." it will be found that the average percentage of discontinuances per year after year 1 is only 2.62, after year 2 it is only 2.17, after year 3 it is 1 87, after year five it is only 1.48, and after this it continues to decrease to 0. When to these facts we add that an equitable, if not liberal cash surrender value, is allowed when a policy has been a few years in force, it will be seen that the frequently made assertion as to immense sums of money being made from lapses is not well founded. Indeed, it is doubtful if the surrender charge much more than compensates an office for the loss of lives which as a rule are healthy and whose loss produces a deterioration on the body of remaining lives. In this connection it is only necessary to refer to Table XX., Part 2, and to the remarks thereon on page 25.

The rate of discontinuance depends not only on the period since entry, but also upon the age at entry. This is made manifest by Table XXV, in which the experience is arranged according to quinquennial ages at entry and quinquennial periods of assurance. From this table it will be seen that the percentage of discontinuances decreases not only with the duration of the assurance, but also with the increase of age at entry. In this table the discontinuances of "year o" are included in those of the first five years, the exposed for "year o" in each group being taken as one-half the number of entrants. A summary of the above-mentioned table is here given :

Ages at Entry.	Per cent. Discontinued. (Whole Duration.)	Duration.	Per cent. Discontinued. (All Ages over 29 Combined.)
20 24	4.88	1st 5 years	7.21
25 29	4.31	2nd "	2.15
30-34	4.16	3rd "	1.19
35 39	3.86	4th "	.80
40-44	3.61	5th "	.68
45 49	3.34	6th "	.50
50 54	3.39	Over 30 years	.50
55 59	3.23		
60 and over.	3.75		
Average	4.14		4.14

The experiences of the Mutual Life of New York and the Australian Mutual Provident Society are also given for convenience in Table XXVI., in groups of quinquennial ages and durations, similar to those in Table XXV. As previously indicated, the function tabulated for these two companies is not quite the same as in the case of the Canada Life ; but what is more important, the matured endowment assurances are included under the head of discontinuances. As the tables stand the proportion of discontinuances is considerably less in the Canada Life than in either of the other two companies, especially in the 3rd, 4th and 5th quinquenniums. The higher rates in the case of the Australian Mutual Provident experience for the later years of assurance are partly accounted for by the matured endowment assurances ; but it is impossible to measure the exact effect of these on the rates of discontinuance. In the Mutual Life experience no term risks had for many years been taken, and very few endowments had matured prior to the close of the observations in 1873, so that the comparison is here more analogous. Moreover, the period of keen competition for new business, and of wide expansion, had not commenced when the Mutual Life experience was taken out. Acting under conditions, therefore, somewhat similar, it appears that the discontinuances in the Canada Life, after the first five years of assurance have been less than in the case of the Mutual Life experience

The importance of separating the compulsory from the voluntary withdrawals in any investigation into the rates of discontinuance has been made manifest, and uncertain if not erroneous results will be brought out where this is not done.

The Diagrams.

The diagrams appended to this report give a graphic illustration of some of the tables already referred to. The first four diagrams are based on Table XIII., and exhibit the relation between the actual deaths in the Canada Life and the expected deaths by the experiences of the Institute of Actuaries (H^m), the American Table, the 30 American Offices, and the Mutual Life of New York, respectively.

Diagrams five to seven illustrate Table XVIII., Part 2, the actual deaths in the experience after five years compared with the corresponding expected deaths by the H^m, Scottish Widows' Fund and Mutual Life Experiences.

Diagram eight, which is based on Table XII., brings into clear view the divergence between the graduated mortality tables of the Institute of Actuaries (H^m), the American Experience, the 30 American Offices, the Mutual Life and Mutual Benefit on the one hand, and the graduated table of the Canada Life on the other.

Conclusion.

In concluding this introduction to the succeeding tables the following considerations suggest themselves :

1. From an examination of the comparative tables already referred to, it appears that the quality of assured male lives in Canada, as evidenced by the Canada Life experience, is not surpassed by that in the United States, Great Britain, Germany or Australia.

2. None of the various individual companies examined and referred to herein show a more favourable mortality experience than the Canada Life Assurance Company.

3. This favourable experience is not confined alone to the early years of assurance, but is maintained when the first five years of assurance are excluded. Indeed, the low rates both of mortality and discontinuance in the period after five years' duration are noticeable characteristics of the present experience.

4. As a consequence of these facts, and of the higher interest rates obtainable in Canada than in most countries, it follows that a well managed Canadian life assurance company possesses special advantages for assurers.

5. Although the rates of mortality at various insuring ages as shown by the Canada Life experience is more favorable than that looked for by the Government

standard, the great caution exercised by the Company in the acceptance of lives and the care manifested in the selection of risks by responsible local agents and medical examiners (a large proportion of whom have acted for the Company for many years and have thus become interested in its permanent welfare), have no doubt largely contributed to the favourable mortality experienced, so that it should not be too hastily assumed that companies and associations in Canada acting under somewhat different conditions would show as favourable a mortality experience as the Canada Life.

6. Moreover, the world-wide decline in the rate of interest in recent years, and the important effect of this on the finance of life assurance, renders it incumbent that the present Government standard should be looked at with both functions (mortality and interest) in view, before any change is adopted.

7. In addition to the publication of the usual aggregate mortality experience, it is hoped the present investigation into the questions of selection and discontinuance, and the publication for proper uses of the complete original facts connected therewith, will do something to advance the interests of actuarial science.

TABLE I. —Continued.

AGE AT ENTRY 19 (Next Birthday.)   NUMBER OF ENTRANTS 227

Years of Assurance	Existing-pied	Mat. pied	With-drawn	Died	Total	Exposed to Risk of Death
			11		11	
1	25	27	1		53	216
2	17	3	2		22	163
3	18	7	1		26	141
4	25	.		1	26	113
5	14	1			15	89
6	10	3			13	74
7	3	4			7	61
8	15				15	54
9	6		.		6	39
10	1	1			2	33
11	1	1	1		3	31
12	4				4	28
13	.		. .			24
14	1		2		3	24
15	1		. .		1	21
16					. .	20
17					. .	20
18					. .	20
19	. .	1	1		1	20
20	1		1	1	2	19
21	. .		. .		. .	17
22	2				2	17
23	3		. .		3	15
24	1		.		1	12
25	1		. .		1	11
26	1		1		2	10
27	1		.		1	8
28	1				1	7
29	1				1	6
30	1				1	5
31	.					4
32			. .			4
33	1		. .		1	4
34			. .			3
35	1		1		2	3
36						1
37						1
38						1
39						1
40						1
41						1
42						1
43	1				1	1
	157	0	62	8	227	1340

AGE AT ENTRY 20 (Next Birthday.)   NUMBER OF ENTRANTS 504

Years of Assurance	Existing	Mat. tured	With-drawn	Died	Total	Exposed to Risk of Death
			23		23	
1	41	81	2		124	481
2	37	11	. .		48	357
3	36	9	1		46	309
4	44	11	1		56	263
5	25	6			31	207
6	24	3			27	176
7	22	4	1		27	149
8	21	2	2		25	122
9	6	3	1		10	97
10	7	1			8	87
11	4	1			5	79
12	8	. .	. .		8	74
13	8	1	1		10	66
14	3	. .	. .		3	56
15	2	1	1		4	53
16	1	1			2	49
17	2	. .			2	47
18	1	1	1		3	45
19	3		.		3	42
20	. .		1		1	39
21	. .		. .		.	38
22	1		1		2	38
23	5		. .		5	36
24	4		. .		4	31
25	5		. .		5	27
26	2		1		3	22
27	3		. .		3	19
28	2		. .		2	16
29			. .			14
30	.		. .		.	14
31	3		1		4	14
32	. .		. .		.	10
33	1				1	10
34	1				1	9
35			1		1	8
36	1				1	7
37	1		1		2	6
38	1				1	4
39					.	3
40	1				1	3
41						2
42						2
43	1				1	2
44						1
45	1				1	1
	328	0	159	17	504	3135

TABLE I. Continued.

AGE AT ENTRY 21 (Next Birthday.) — NUMBER OF ENTRANTS 1503

Years of Assurance	Existing.	Measured.	Withdrawn.	Died.	Total.	Exposed to Risk of Death.
	..	..	47	..	47	
1	80	1	220	3	304	1456
2	52	..	57	11	120	1152
3	58	..	57	7	122	1032
4	110	1	36	3	150	910
5	47	..	36	9	92	760
6	64	..	19	7	87	668
7	42	..	15	6	63	581
8	43	..	12	4	59	518
9	43	..	8	3	54	459
10	54	..	7	3	64	405
11	41	..	2	6	49	341
12	28	..	3	..	31	292
13	23	..	1	2	26	261
14	25	..	2	1	28	235
15	30	..	..	..	30	207
16	19	..	1	3	23	177
17	22	..	..	1	23	154
18	18	..	1	3	22	131
19	16	1	2	..	19	109
20	16	..	..	1	17	90
21	20	..	..	..	20	73
22	16	..	1	..	17	53
23	14	..	..	..	14	36
24	5	..	1	..	6	22
25	..	..	..	..	.	16
26	1	..	..	..	1	16
27	1	..	..	2	3	15
28	..	..	..	..	..	12
29	2	..	..	..	2	12
30	..	1	..	..	1	10
31	..	..	..	..		9
32	2	..	..	..	2	9
33	2	..	1	..	3	7
34	..	..	..	..		4
35	1	..	..	..	1	4
36	..	..	..	..		3
37	1	..	..	..	1	3
38	..	..	..	..		2
39	1	..	..	..	1	2
40	1	..	..	..	1	1
	895	4	529	75	1503	10247

AGE AT ENTRY 22 (Next Birthday.) — NUMBER OF ENTRANTS 1508.

Years of Assurance	Existing.	Measured.	Withdrawn.	Died.	Total.	Exposed to Risk of Death.
	..	..	68	..	68	
1	86	..	240	6	332	1440
2	53	..	81	6	140	1108
3	66	..	45	8	119	968
4	75	..	34	6	115	849
5	46	..	30	8	84	734
6	42	..	17	1	60	650
7	61	..	18	2	81	590
8	47	..	11	5	63	509
9	37	..	7	3	47	446
10	33	..	8	1	42	399
11	31	..	3	2	36	357
12	33	..	5	3	41	321
13	28	..	4	2	34	280
14	28	..	4	1	33	246
15	28	..	2	1	31	213
16	14	..	2	..	16	182
17	18	..	..	3	21	166
18	19	..	1	2	22	145
19	12	..	1	3	16	123
20	9	..	..	1	10	107
21	22	..	..	..	22	97
22	16	..	1	..	17	75
23	18	..	..	..	18	58
24	11	..	..	..	11	40
25	6	..	..	1	7	29
26	2	..	..	1	3	22
27	1	..	..	..	1	19
28	2	..	..	1	3	18
29	1	..	..	..	1	15
30	1	..	..	1	2	14
31	3	..	..	..	3	12
32	2	..	..	..	2	9
33	2	..	..	..	2	7
34	2	..	..	..	2	5
35	..	..	..	..		3
36	..	..	..	..		3
37	..	..	..	..	..	3
38	..	..	..	1	1	3
39	..	..	..	..		2
40	..	..	..	..		2
41	..	..	..	..		2
42	..	..	..	..		2
43	..	..	..	..		2
44	1	..	..	1	2	2
	856	0	583	69	1508	10277

TABLE I.

	AGE AT ENTRY 15 (Next Birthday)							AGE AT ENTRY 16 (Next Birthday)					
Years of Assurance	NUMBER OF ENTRANTS 5						**Years of Assurance**	NUMBER OF ENTRANTS 14					
	Existing	Matured	Withdrawn	Died	Total	Exposed to Risk of Death		Existing	Matured	Withdrawn	Died	Total	Exposed to Risk of Death
1						5	1	2		2		1	14
2			..		..	5	2	2		1		3	10
3			2		2	5	3			1		1	7
4			1		1	3	4						6
5						2	5						6
6						2	6	1				1	6
7						2	7			1		1	5
8						2	8					..	4
9						2	9						4
10						2	10						4
11						2	11						4
12						2	12						4
13						2	13						4
14						2	14						4
15						2	15						4
16			1	1		2	16						3
17						2	17						4
18						2	18						4
19						2	19				1	1	4
20						2	20						3
21	1		1			2	21	..					3
22		1				2	22	..				..	3
23				1		2	23	1				1	3
24				1		2	24	1				1	2
25				1		2	25	1				1	1
26		1				2							
27						2							
28						2							
29						2							
30			1		1	2							
31						1							
32						1							
33						1							
34						1							
35						1							
36						1							
37						1							
38						1							
39						1							
40						1							
41						1							
42						1							
43	1			1		1							
	1	0	4	0	5	83		8	0	5	1	14	117

TABLE I. —Continued.

AGE AT ENTRY 17 (Next Birthday.)   AGE AT ENTRY 18 (Next Birthday.)

Year of Assurance	NUMBER OF ENTRANTS 37						Year of Assurance	NUMBER OF ENTRANTS 92					
	Existing	Matured	With-drawn.	Died.	Total.	Exposed to Risk of Death.		Existing	Matured	With-drawn.	Died.	Total.	Exposed to Risk of Death.
	..		..		11	37		..		2	..	2	90
1	2		4		11	37	1	9		11		20	90
2	1		1		2	26	2	9		4		13	70
3	5		2		7	24	3	3		3	1	7	57
4	2		1		3	17	4	10		..		10	50
5	1		1		2	14	5	4		..		4	40
6	1				1	12	6	..		1		1	36
7					11	11	7	4		..		4	35
8	3				3	11	8	3				3	31
9					8	8	9	1		..		1	28
10					8	8	10	..		1		1	27
11					8	8	11	1		..		1	26
12					8	8	12	1		1		2	25
13					8	8	13					..	23
14					8	8	14					..	23
15					8	8	15					..	23
16			..		..	8	16				1	1	23
17			1		1	8	17				1	1	22
18			..	1	1	7	18	1		..	1	2	21
19						6	19	..		..	..	..	19
20						6	20		..	..		..	19
21						6	21		..	1	..	1	19
22					..	6	22		..			..	18
23						6	23	2		..		2	18
24	2	..			2	6	24	4	..			4	16
25					..	4	25	..	..		1	1	12
26	1				1	4	26	1	..	1	1	3	11
27	1				1	3	27	1		..		1	8
28		..				2	28	1	..			1	7
29		..				2	29	1		..		1	6
30						2	30	..				..	5
31						2	31					..	5
32						2	32		..			..	5
33						2	33		..			..	5
34						2	34		..			..	5
35						2	35					..	5
36						2	36	1				1	5
37						2	37	1	..			1	4
38						2	38	1		1		2	3
39						2	39					..	1
40					..	2	40					..	1
41				1	1	2	41					..	1
42					..	1	42	1				1	1
43						1							
44					..	1							
45	1				1	1							
	25	0	10	2	37	307		60	0	26	6	92	849

TABLE I. Continued.

AGE AT ENTRY 23 (Next Birthday.) — NUMBER OF ENTRANTS 1708

Years of Assurance	Existing	Matured	Withdrawn	Died	Total	Exposed to Risk of Death
			72		72	
1	95		253	4	352	1636
2	60		80	8	148	1284
3	63		53	5	121	1136
4	80		44	5	129	1015
5	62		39	2	103	886
6	42		21	4	67	783
7	52		20	5	77	716
8	46		11	8	65	639
9	43		11	4	58	574
10	43	1	8	4	56	516
11	44		6	1	54	460
12	30		9	5	53	406
13	35		8	4	47	353
14	31		4	4	39	306
15	35		3	1	39	267
16	19			3	22	228
17	19			2	21	206
18	19		3	3	25	185
19	24		1	1	26	160
20	12		2	1	15	134
21	15			1	16	119
22	27				27	103
23	12			2	14	76
24	8		1		9	62
25	10		1	2	13	53
26	3			2	5	40
27	4				4	35
28	1		1		2	31
29	4				4	29
30	1				1	25
31	1			1	5	24
32	1				1	19
33	2				2	18
34	2				2	16
35						14
36	3				3	14
37						11
38	3				3	11
39						8
40	3				3	8
41	1		1		2	5
42						3
43	1				1	
44						
45	2				2	
	970	1	651	83	1708	12621

AGE AT ENTRY 24 (Next Birthday) — NUMBER OF ENTRANTS 1725

Years of Assurance	Existing	Matured	Withdrawn	Died	Total	Exposed to Risk of Death
			66		66	
1	73		263	6	342	1659
2	65		106	10	181	1317
3	56		61	5	122	1136
4	79		26	3	108	1014
5	47		36	6	89	966
6	51		12	5	68	817
7	56		19	8	83	749
8	34		16	1	51	666
9	44		13	4	61	615
10	43		9	4	56	554
11	42		6	3	51	498
12	46		3	3	52	447
13	41		6	3	50	345
14	29		4	2	35	345
15	30		2	1	33	310
16	15		3	5	23	277
17	21		2	3	26	254
18	22			2	24	228
19	34		2	2	38	204
20	30			3	33	166
21	23		1	3	27	133
22	15		1	1	20	106
23	13				13	86
24	4				4	73
25	7				7	69
26	9	1		1	11	62
27	9				9	51
28	4				3	42
29	2			1	3	38
30	3			2	5	35
31	3				3	30
32	1				1	27
33	2				2	26
34	2			1	3	24
35	2				2	21
36	1				4	19
37						15
38	1		1		1	14
39	1				1	13
40						12
41	2				2	12
42	3				2	10
43	2					
44						
45	3					
	973	1	658	93	1725	13486

TABLE I.—Continued.

AGE AT ENTRY 25 (Next Birthday.)

NUMBER OF ENTRANTS 1765.

Years of Assurance	Existing	Matured	Withdrawn	Died	Total	Exposed to Risk of Death.
	..	..	67	..	67	
1	78	..	278	6	362	1698
2	54	..	88	9	151	1336
3	54	..	52	6	112	1185
4	84	..	36	2	122	1073
5	56	..	29	6	91	951
6	42	..	30	3	75	860
7	35	..	18	6	59	785
8	51	..	13	4	68	726
9	54	..	9	3	66	658
10	44	..	11	6	61	592
11	44	..	7	2	53	531
12	54	..	5	2	61	478
13	51	..	6	3	60	417
14	31	..	3	1	35	357
15	27	..	4	1	32	322
16	27	..	..	4	31	290
17	25	..	2	2	29	259
18	22	..	1	1	24	230
19	20	..	2	1	23	206
20	18	..	..	1	19	183
21	29	..	1	1	31	164
22	26	..	2	..	28	133
23	19	..	2	1	22	105
24	9	..	..	1	10	83
25	13	1	1	2	17	73
26	4	..	2	..	6	56
27	4	..	..	..	4	50
28	4	..	1	1	6	46
29	6	..	..	1	7	40
30	2	..	1	2	5	33
31	3	..	1	..	4	28
32	3	..	..	..	3	24
33	6	..	..	..	6	21
34	..	..	1	..	1	15
35	1	..	..	..	1	14
36	1	..	..	..	1	13
37	1	..	..	..	1	12
38	1	..	..	..	1	11
39	2	..	..	..	2	10
40	1	..	..	1	2	8
41	..	..	..	..	..	6
42	1	..	..	..	1	6
43	..	..	..	1	1	5
44	2	..	..	..	2	4
45	2	..	..	..	2	2
	1011	1	673	80	1765	14099

AGE AT ENTRY 26 (Next Birthday.)

NUMBER OF ENTRANTS 1730.

Years of Assurance	Existing	Matured	Withdrawn	Died	Total	Exposed to Risk of Death.
	..	..	55	..	55	
1	78	..	281	6	365	1675
2	41	1	99	6	147	1310
3	46	1	66	8	121	1163
4	80	..	31	8	119	1042
5	56	..	38	..	94	923
6	47	..	25	1	73	829
7	39	..	12	6	57	756
8	36	..	11	2	49	699
9	55	..	12	8	75	650
10	57	..	12	2	71	575
11	34	..	6	3	43	504
12	53	..	9	6	68	461
13	46	..	3	4	53	393
14	26	..	3	2	31	340
15	21	..	4	3	28	309
16	23	..	1	1	25	281
17	23	..	3	..	26	256
18	27	..	3	3	33	230
19	28	..	6	2	36	197
20	22	..	1	2	25	161
21	20	..	3	3	26	136
22	15	..	..	3	18	110
23	25	..	2	..	27	92
24	7	..	..	1	8	65
25	4	..	1	1	6	57
26	7	..	..	1	8	51
27	2	..	1	..	3	43
28	8	..	..	..	8	40
29	3	..	..	2	5	32
30	1	..	..	1	2	27
31	2	..	..	3	5	25
32	2	..	..	..	2	20
33	3	..	1	..	4	18
34	1	..	1	2	4	14
35	..	..	..	..	..	10
36	1	..	..	..	1	10
37	2	..	..	..	2	9
38	..	..	..	1	1	7
39	1	..	..	1	2	6
40	3	..	..	..	3	4
41	1	..	..	..	1	1
	946	2	690	92	1730	13531

TABLE I.—Continued.

AGE AT ENTRY 27 (Next Birthday.)

NUMBER OF ENTRANTS 1762

Years of Assurance	Existing	Matured	Withdrawn	Died	Total	Exposed to Risk of Death
			75		75	
1	79		263	8	350	1687
2	48		101	7	156	1337
3	50		71	3	124	1181
4	66		26	5	97	1057
5	50		34	5	98	960
6	41		18	3	62	862
7	40		18	6	64	800
8	47		16	1	67	736
9	48		5	7	60	669
10	47		5	1	53	609
11	48		6	4	58	556
12	39		10	3	52	498
13	47		3	1	51	446
14	40		5	1	55	395
15	13		5	2	20	340
16	25		3	2	30	320
17	26		1	2	29	290
18	23		1	1	25	261
19	26		2	4	32	236
20	22		2	1	25	204
21	16		2	2	20	179
22	18		1	3	22	159
23	30	3	2	1	36	137
24	9		1	1	11	101
25	9			2	11	90
26	7				7	79
27	2				7	72
28	1				1	65
29	6		3	1	10	64
30	3		1		4	54
31	5				5	50
32	5			1	6	45
33	9			1	10	39
34	2			2	4	29
35	1				1	25
36	1				1	24
37	3				3	23
38	3			1	4	20
39	1				1	16
40	3			2	5	15
41	2			1	3	10
42						7
43	3				3	7
44	2				2	4
45	2				2	2
	991	3	680	88	1762	14760

AGE AT ENTRY 28 (Next Birthday.)

NUMBER OF ENTRANTS 1738.

Years of Assurance	Existing	Matured	Withdrawn	Died	Total	Exposed to Risk of Death
			63		63	
1	78	2	238	2	320	1675
2	52		85	5	142	1355
3	44		68	8	120	1213
4	68		39	4	111	1093
5	37		35	2	74	982
6	51		24	8	83	908
7	36		16	6	68	825
8	51		18	9	78	757
9	49		11	9	69	679
10	46		11	4	61	610
11	43		8	5	56	549
12	46		2	3	51	493
13	48		6	7	61	412
14	26		4	1	31	381
15	29		3	1	33	350
16	19		3	1	23	317
17	20		1	2	23	294
18	22		2	1	25	271
19	24		1	1	26	246
20	19		2	5	26	220
21	33		3	3	39	194
22	28	3		1	32	155
23	33			3	36	123
24	6			2	8	87
25	10			1	11	79
26	9			3	12	68
27	6				6	56
28	2			1	3	50
29	2			1	3	47
30	2			1	3	44
31	1			2	3	41
32	3			1	4	38
33	9				9	34
34	2				2	25
35	2				2	23
36	1				1	21
37	3			1	4	20
38	3			1	4	16
39	3				3	12
40	1				1	9
41	5				5	8
42						3
43	1				1	3
44						2
45	2				2	2
	985	5	643	105	1738	14820

TABLE I.—Continued.

AGE AT ENTRY 29 (Next Birthday.) — NUMBER OF ENTRANTS 1655.

Years of Assurance	Existing	Matured	Withdrawn	Died	Total	Exposed to Risk of Death.
	..	..	57	..	57	
1	72	..	224	1	297	1598
2	52	..	87	9	148	1301
3	57	..	49	10	116	1153
4	73	..	34	5	112	1037
5	40	..	36	3	79	925
6	37	..	20	6	63	846
7	35	..	16	7	58	783
8	44	..	12	4	60	725
9	37	..	6	7	50	665
10	37	1	5	3	46	615
11	48	1	10	4	63	569
12	51	..	4	5	60	506
13	46	..	7	4	57	446
14	35	..	4	3	42	389
15	30	..	4	1	35	347
16	26	..	7	3	36	312
17	24	..	2	1	27	276
18	21	..	2	1	24	249
19	25	..	..	3	28	225
20	14	..	..	2	16	197
21	27	2	2	3	34	181
22	14	..	1	2	17	147
23	17	..	1	..	18	130
24	14	..	.	1	15	112
25	6	..	1	2	9	97
26	5	..	..	4	9	88
27	5	..	1	4	10	79
28	6	..	..	1	7	69
29	6	..	1	1	8	62
30	3	..	..	2	5	54
31	3	..	1	2	6	49
32	4	1	..	2	7	43
33	4	..	..	2	6	36
34	5	..	..	2	7	30
35	3	..	..	..	3	23
36	1	..	..	..	1	20
37	2	..	..	..	2	19
38	1	..	..	1	2	17
39	1	..	..	1	2	15
40	2	..	..	..	2	13
41	1	..	..	1	2	11
42	3	..	..	..	3	9
43	3	..	..	..	3	6
44	..	..	..	..	..	3
45	2	..	..	..	2	3
46	1	..	..	..	1	1
	943	5	594	113	1655	14481

AGE AT ENTRY 30 (Next Birthday.) — NUMBER OF ENTRANTS 1587.

Years of Assurance	Existing	Matured	Withdrawn	Died	Total	Exposed to Risk of Death.
	..	.	50	..	50	
1	70	..	217	4	291	1537
2	53	..	83	6	142	1246
3	49	..	50	4	103	1104
4	46	..	28	8	82	1001
5	41	..	34	3	78	919
6	38	..	28	6	72	841
7	46	..	31	6	83	769
8	49	..	15	2	66	686
9	41	..	13	1	55	620
10	42	..	5	6	53	565
11	25	..	1	7	33	512
12	43	..	5	5	53	479
13	40	..	6	..	46	426
14	31	..	3	4	38	380
15	20	..	5	7	32	342
16	20	..	2	5	27	310
17	27	..	4	5	36	283
18	21	..	3	3	27	247
19	16	..	5	3	24	220
20	19	5	1	..	25	196
21	19	3	..	3	25	171
22	20	..	2	..	22	146
23	16	..	1	2	19	124
24	15	..	2	3	20	105
25	9	..	1	1	11	85
26	6	..	..	1	7	74
27	4	..	..	1	5	67
28	4	..	..	1	5	62
29	5	..	..	1	6	57
30	2	1	..	2	5	51
31	4	..	..	..	4	46
32	6	..	1	1	8	42
33	2	..	..	..	2	34
34	3	..	1	3	7	32
35	..	..	..	..	..	25
36	2	..	1	1	4	25
37	2	..	..	..	2	21
38	2	..	..	..	2	19
39	4	..	..	..	4	17
40	2	..	..	1	3	13
41	..	..	..	1	1	10
42	3	..	..	..	3	9
43	1	..	..	..	1	6
44	1	..	..	1	2	5
45	1	..	..	..	1	3
46	2	..	..	..	2	2
	872	9	598	108	1587	13934

TABLE I. Continued.

AGE AT ENTRY 31 (Next Birthday)   AGE AT ENTRY 32 (Next Birthday)

Years of Assurance	NUMBER OF ENTRANTS 1619						Years of Assurance	NUMBER OF ENTRANTS 1516					
	Existing	Matured	Withdrawn	Died	Total	Expected Risk of Deaths		Existing	Matured	Withdrawn	Died	Total	Expected Risk of Deaths
			64		64					63		63	
1	60		211	1	314	1355	1	61		219	2	282	1435
2	58		89	7	154	1241	2	40		77	8	125	1171
3	39		54	1	104	1087	3	33		50	7	92	1046
4	63		32	7	102	983	4	53		10	5	98	956
5	37		38	6	81	881	5	42		24	3	60	858
6	56		23	5	64	800	6	35		23	1	59	780
7	47	1	21	3	72	736	7	37		17	3	57	730
8	34		18	5	57	664	8	33		13	5	51	673
9	36		9	1	46	607	9	44		11	6	61	622
10	33	3	5	3	54	561	10	42	1	5	1	52	561
11	38		3	5	46	507	11	25		6	3	33	609
12	40	1	3	2	48	461	12	44		6	3	53	475
13	33		4	1	30	443	13	34		6	3	43	422
14	29		4	3	36	374	14	35		5	2	42	379
15	15		3		18	338	15	20		1	3	21	337
16	22		2	3	27	320	16	16		3	1	23	343
17	26		2	5	33	293	17	14		2	1	20	290
18	26		1		27	260	18	15	1	1	2	22	270
19	17	4	1	1	23	233	19	28	1		2	31	247
20	23	2	2	1	28	210	20	20		2	1	26	217
21	31		2		33	182	21	25		3		28	191
22	17			2	19	149	22	19		3		22	163
23	25			2	27	130	23	17	1	2	3	23	131
24	13	1		3	17	103	24	13	1		1	15	118
25	7			3	10	86	25	4			3	7	103
26	7		3		10	70	26	10		1	1	12	92
27	6		1	1	8	66	27	13			2	15	84
28	2		1	3	38	58	28	8		1	4	9	69
29	6	1		3	10	55	29	2	1		2	5	60
30	3	1	1		5	45	30	4			1	5	55
31	2		2	1		40	31	4		1		5	50
32	1		1	2	7	36	32	5		1	1	7	45
33	5		4		20	20	33	4		3		38	38
34	3		2	5	20	20	34	3		4		31	31
35	2			2	15	15	35	1		1		25	25
36	4			1	13	13	36	2			2	23	23
37					12	12	37	5			3	21	21
38	1			1	12	12	38	2				16	16
39					11	11	39	1				14	14
40	1		2	3	11	11	40	3			1	13	13
41	1		1	5	8	8	41			1	1	10	10
42						3	42	1			1	9	9
43	2			2	5	5	43			1	1	8	8
44	1			1	1	1	44	3				5	7
45							45	3				3	3
46							46	1				1	1
	885	14	625	95	1619	13688		824	9	578	105	1516	13714

TABLE I.—Continued.

AGE AT ENTRY 33 (Next Birthday.)

NUMBER OF ENTRANTS 1378.

Years of Assurance	Existing	Ma-tured	With-drawn	Died	Total	Exposed to Risk of Death
			30		50	
1	37		204	3	244	1328
2	45		71	6	125	1084
3	40		42	4	86	959
4	50		27	9	86	873
5	36	1	26	5	68	787
6	30		30	6	66	719
7	30		14	8	52	653
8	26		17	7	50	601
9	36		12	5	53	551
10	30		7	2	39	498
11	26		5	2	33	459
12	35		5	13	53	426
13	35		3	3	41	373
14	26			2	28	332
15	25		9	3	37	304
16	21		4	3	28	267
17	12	3	1	4	20	239
18	24	1	2	1	28	219
19	8		1	1	10	191
20	22		5		27	181
21	22		2	1	23	154
22	19		3	2	25	131
23	13				13	106
24	13		1	1	15	93
25	4				4	78
26	4			2	6	74
27	10	2			12	68
28	1	1	1	2	5	56
29	1		1	3	5	51
30	2		1	3	6	46
31	6			7	7	40
32	2			1	3	33
33	2			1	3	30
34					27	27
35	1			3	4	27
36	1			2	3	23
37	2			1	20	20
38	3			2	5	16
39			1		1	11
40	1			1	1	10
41	2				2	9
42	2				2	7
43	1				1	5
44	1				1	4
45	2			1	3	3
	707	8	549	114	1378	12166

AGE AT ENTRY 34 (Next Birthday.)

NUMBER OF ENTRANTS 1278.

Years of Assurance	Existing	Ma-tured	With-drawn	Died	Total	Exposed to Risk of Death
			40		40	
1	45	1	154	4	204	1238
2	35		74	4	113	1034
3	40		52	12	104	921
4	41		31	6	78	817
5	29		24	7	60	739
6	25	1	17	3	46	679
7	38		18	4	60	633
8	38		14	4	56	573
9	34		10	2	46	517
10	35	2	6	7	50	471
11	28		8	2	38	421
12	24		3	4	31	383
13	30		7	3	40	352
14	21		8	2	31	312
15	17		2	7	26	281
16	12	1	1	5	19	255
17	21	1	2	1	25	236
18	14		3	5	22	211
19	5			4	9	189
20	21			1	22	180
21	18	4		4	26	158
22	20	1	2	1	24	132
23	14		3	2	19	108
24	8		1	3	12	89
25	8			1	9	77
26	3	1		2	6	68
27	9			3	12	62
28	6			1	7	50
29	3			4	7	43
30	1		1	4	6	36
31	1				1	30
32	3				3	29
33	3				3	26
34	1			1	2	23
35	1			1	2	21
36	4				4	19
37	1			1	2	15
38	2				2	13
39	1			2	6	11
40	1			1	2	5
41	1				1	3
42	1				1	2
43						1
44	1				1	1
	667	12	481	118	1278	11464

TABLE I. Continued.

Years of Assurance	NUMBER OF ENTRANTS 1231					Years of Assurance	NUMBER OF ENTRANTS 1145				
	Existing	Matured	Withdrawn	Died	Total	Exposed to Risk of Death		Existing	Matured	Withdrawn	Died	Total	Exposed to Risk of Death
			41		41					49		49	
1	40		151	2	193	1190	1	39		151	5	198	1099
2	30	3	64	2	105	997	2	24		68	2	99	901
3	33		36	4	70	892	3	41		38	3	82	802
4	39		30	4	73	822	4	40		26	4	70	720
5	44		28	6	76	749	5	29		19	4	52	650
6	19		23	8	50	671	6	29		15	6	50	598
7	20		15	6	40	621	7	22		13	2	37	548
8	23		13	2	38	572	8	28		11	6	45	511
9	33		9	5	47	534	9	34		6	4	44	466
10	32		8	2	42	487	10	25	1	5	4	35	422
11	27		7	7	41	445	11	28		5	3	34	387
12	37		9	5	51	404	12	29		7	3	39	353
13	24		5	2	31	353	13	34		5	1	40	314
14	18		7	7	32	322	14	19	2	1	1	23	274
15	27	3	2	6	38	290	15	22		6	4	32	251
16	17		6	1	24	252	16	10		3	2	15	229
17	18		2	3	23	228	17	16		2	2	20	204
18	21		1	5	27	205	18	17		3	3	23	184
19	14			3	17	178	19	13	1	1		15	161
20	17	3	2	2	24	161	20	10	2	2	3	17	146
21	13	2	1	1	30	137	21	17			1	18	130
22	27		2	2	31	117	22	17			1	18	111
23	15	1	1	1	18	86	23	14			2	16	93
24	5			1	9	68	24	11	1	1	1	14	77
25	3	3	1	1	13	59	25	5			4	9	63
26	5				5	46	26	4			1	5	54
27	2			3	10	41	27	2			5	7	49
28	1		1	2	4	31	28	4				4	42
29				1	2	27	29	3	1			4	38
30	2		1		3	25	30	2			2	4	34
31	1			1		22	31	4			1	5	30
32	6			3	9	21	32	3		1		4	25
33						12	33	2			1	3	21
34						17	34	1				1	18
35				1	1	12	35	1			2	3	17
36	2			2		11	36	1			1	2	14
37				1	1	9	37	1			1	2	12
38	2				5	8	38	2				1	10
39	2				2	6	39	1			2	3	8
40	1				4	4	40	2			2	4	5
41						3	41						1
42						3	42						1
43	1				1	5	43						1
44	1				1	2	44	1				1	1
45	1				1	1							
	649	15	466	101	1231	11139		605	8	435	97	1145	10005

TABLE I. Continued.

AGE AT ENTRY 37 (Next Birthday.)

NUMBER OF ENTRANTS 1077.

Years of Assurance	Existing	Matured	Withdrawn	Died	Total	Exposed to Risk of Death
	..	..	33	..	33	
1	36	..	146	2	184	1044
2	37	1	62	4	104	860
3	28	1	30	..	59	756
4	36		24	3	63	697
5	26		19	5	50	634
6	24		13	6	43	584
7	36		12	4	52	541
8	23		9	4	36	489
9	22		6	2	30	453
10	31		4	7	42	423
11	18		7	1	26	381
12	28		4	2	34	355
13	25		3	1	29	321
14	22		2	5	29	292
15	25		4	7	36	263
16	15		1		16	227
17	14		2	3	19	211
18	13		1	1	15	192
19	9	2	..		11	177
20	12		3	4	18	166
21	19		1	2	22	148
22	18		2	4	24	126
23	23	2		6	31	102
24	7	1	..		9	71
25	4		1		5	62
26	6		1	1	8	57
27	..			4	4	49
28	3			1	4	45
29	2			2	4	41
30	1			1	2	37
31	1			1	5	35
32	3		..	1	4	30
33			1	1	2	26
34	1			2	3	24
35						21
36				1	1	21
37				2	2	20
38	1		..	1	1	18
39			1	3	4	17
40	3		..		3	13
41	2		1		3	10
42	3				3	7
43	2			1	3	4
44					1	1
45	1				1	1
	583	**7**	**392**	**95**	**1077**	**10052**

AGE AT ENTRY 38 (Next Birthday.)

NUMBER OF ENTRANTS 990.

Years of Assurance	Existing	Matured	Withdrawn	Died	Total	Exposed to Risk of Death
	..		40		40	
1	36		123	2	161	950
2	28		63	3	94	789
3	28		24	5	57	695
4	36		19	3	58	638
5	25		19	1	45	580
6	18		13	4	35	535
7	23		16		39	500
8	23		14	6	43	461
9	15		3	3	21	418
10	24		8	3	35	397
11	22		6	2	30	362
12	21		6	..	27	332
13	25		1	2	28	305
14	17		1	4	25	277
15	20		1	4	28	252
16	19		2		21	224
17	16	2	1	2	21	203
18	15	1		3	19	182
19	15			2	17	163
20	14	..	1	3	18	146
21	11		1	5	17	128
22	21	..	2	3	26	111
23	14	1	1	3	19	85
24	9		1	2	12	66
25	3				3	54
26	6			1	7	51
27	8			1	6	44
28	1				1	35
29	2			4	6	34
30	..					28
31	2			1	3	28
32	3		1	1	5	25
33	3			2	5	20
34	..					15
35	1				1	15
36	1			2	3	11
37	2			1	3	11
38	2			1	3	8
39						5
40	1				1	5
41				1	1	1
42				1	1	3
43	..			1	1	2
44	1				1	1
	531	**4**	**373**	**82**	**990**	**9201**

TABLE I. Continued.

AGE AT ENTRY 39 (Next Birthday.)

NUMBER OF ENTRANTS 860.

Years of Assurance	Existing	Matured	Withdrawn	Died	Total	Exposed to Risk of Death
			27		27	
1	31	1	104	5	141	833
2	25		38	4	67	692
3	21		51	4	56	625
4	33		20	6	59	569
5	10		17	2	39	510
6	20		14	6	40	471
7	33		7	2	42	431
8	21		4	2	27	389
9	21		7	4	32	362
10	25		4	5	34	330
11	18		3	3	24	296
12	22		3	1	26	272
13	17			3	20	246
14	17		3	2	22	226
15	10			5	15	204
16	10	3	1	6	20	189
17	10		2	2	14	169
18	13		1	2	16	155
19	7			3	10	139
20	10			1	11	129
21	21	2	1	3	27	118
22	20		2	3	25	91
23	9			2	11	66
24	3				3	55
25	4			1	5	52
26	3			1	4	47
27	2			1	3	43
28	2			4	6	40
29	2			2	4	34
30	2			2	4	30
31	1			2	3	26
32	2				2	23
33	2			1	3	21
34						18
35	1				1	18
36	1			2	3	17
37	2				2	14
38				1	1	12
39	2				2	11
40	1				1	9
41	1				1	8
42	2				2	7
43	1		1		2	5
44	1		1		2	3
45	1				1	1
	470	6	289	95	800	8000

AGE AT ENTRY 40 (Next Birthday.)

NUMBER OF ENTRANTS 815

Years of Assurance	Existing	Matured	Withdrawn	Died	Total	Exposed to Risk of Death
			23		23	
1	31	1	83	1	116	792
2	29		33	1	65	676
3	19	1	26	5	51	611
4	33		15	8	56	560
5	18	1	20	2	41	504
6	21		9	3	33	463
7	26		8	5	39	430
8	22		9	7	38	391
9	21	1	5	2	29	353
10	21	1	4	2	28	324
11	21		6		27	296
12	28		2	4	34	269
13	27		2	1	30	235
14	20		1	1	22	205
15	10		3	2	15	183
16	4		5	3	12	168
17	11		1	2	14	156
18	9		2	4	15	142
19	11		1	3	15	127
20	11	7	1	4	23	112
21	10	1	1		12	89
22	14			2	16	77
23	11			1	12	61
24	6			1	7	49
25	2			1	3	42
26	5				5	39
27	7				7	34
28	1				1	32
29	1			2	3	31
30	2			1	3	28
31	1				1	25
32	4			3	7	24
33	2			3	5	17
34			1	1	2	12
35				1	1	10
36	1				1	9
37	1				1	8
38						7
39	3				3	7
40	2				2	4
41	1				1	2
42						1
43	1					1
	463	13	263	76	815	7000

TABLE I.—Continued.

AGE AT ENTRY 41 (Next Birthday.)

Years of Assurance	NUMBER OF ENTRANTS 740.					
	Existing	Matured	With-drawn	Died	Total	Exposed to Risk of Death.
	..	..	19	..	19	
1	33	..	90	3	126	724
2	24	..	37	2	63	595
3	19	..	23	4	46	532
4	32	..	15	..	37	486
5	12	..	14	3	29	439
6	21	..	20	2	43	410
7	15	..	13	3	31	367
8	23	..	8	2	33	336
9	16	..	6	2	24	303
10	15	..	2	1	18	279
11	18	..	7	5	30	261
12	18	1	..	1	20	231
13	13	..	2	4	19	211
14	20	..	3	2	25	192
15	12	..	1	6	19	167
16	11	..	1	3	15	148
17	6	..	3	3	12	133
18	7	..	..	1	8	121
19	7	4	..	4	13	113
20	7	3	..	1	12	98
21	12	..	1	3	16	87
22	6	..	..	2	8	71
23	10	..	1	..	11	63
24	9	..	..	2	11	52
25	2	..	1	2	5	41
26	1	..	..	..	1	36
27	2	..	..	3	5	35
28	1	..	..	2	3	30
29	1	..	..	2	3	27
30	..	..	..	..		24
31	2	..	..	1	3	24
32	1	..	..	1	2	21
33	1	..	..	3	4	19
34	..	..	..	..		15
35	..	..	..	1	1	15
36	2	..	..	..	2	14
37	..	..	..	2	2	12
38	..	..	..	..		10
39	1	..	..	3	4	10
40	1	..	..	..	1	6
41	1	..	..	2	3	5
42	1	..	..	..	1	2
43	..	..	..	1	1	1
	383	8	267	82	740	6763

AGE AT ENTRY 42 (Next Birthday.)

Years of Assurance	NUMBER OF ENTRANTS 656.					
	Existing	Matured	With-drawn	Died	Total	Exposed to Risk of Death.
	..	..	24	..	24	
1	25	1	77	5	108	632
2	14	..	39	1	54	524
3	24	..	19	3	46	470
4	22	..	13	2	37	424
5	18	..	11	1	30	387
6	14	..	8	6	28	357
7	25	1	12	3	41	329
8	15	..	5	1	21	288
9	15	..	2	3	20	267
10	16	..	3	1	20	247
11	16	..	3	6	25	227
12	14	..	..	1	15	202
13	16	..	1	3	20	187
14	17	..	1	5	23	167
15	7	..	..	1	8	144
16	14	..	1	2	17	136
17	10	..	1	2	13	119
18	11	1	2	1	15	106
19	4	1	1	2	8	91
20	11	..	1	1	13	83
21	7	..	1	4	12	70
22	8	..	..	5	13	58
23	7	..	..	..	7	45
24	2	..	..	1	3	38
25	1	..	..	2	3	35
26	1	..	..	..	1	32
27	5	..	..	1	6	31
28	2	..	..	3	5	25
29	2	..	..	..	2	20
30	1	..	1	2	4	18
31	..	..	..	1	1	14
32	2	..	..	..	2	13
33	1	..	..	..	1	11
34	..	..	..	..		10
35	..	..	..	..		10
36	2	..	..	..	2	10
37	1	..	..	1	2	8
38	..	..	..	..		6
39	..	..	..	..		6
40	2	..	..	..	2	6
41	1	..	..	..	1	4
42	..	..	..	1	1	3
43	..	..	..	1	1	2
44	1	..	..	..	1	1
	354	4	226	72	656	5863

TABLE 1. Continued.

AGE AT ENTRY 43 (Next Birthday)

NUMBER OF ENTRANTS 590

Years of Assurance	Existing	Matured	Withdrawn	Died	Total	Exposed to Risk of Death
	..		15		15	
1	21		86		107	575
2	14		30	2	46	468
3	19	..	12	2	33	422
4	18	..	7	4	29	389
5	9	1	14	3	27	360
6	16		10	2	22	333
7	11	..	14	5	30	311
8	12		4	5	21	281
9	11	..	3	6	20	260
10	14	..	2	2	18	240
11	15	..	2	2	19	222
12	13	1	1	3	18	203
13	17	1	..	..	18	185
14	16		1	1	18	167
15	9	..	..	2	11	149
16	11	..	1	1	13	138
17	9	1	..	1	11	125
18	10	2	..	3	15	114
19	7	..	..	2	9	99
20	11	..	..	2	13	90
21	10	..	..	4	14	77
22	12	..	..	..	12	63
23	8	..	..	3	11	51
24	4		..	2	6	40
25	3		..	2	5	34
26	5		..	2	7	29
27	2		..	2	4	22
28	2	..		..	2	18
29	1	..		2	3	16
30	..	..		1	1	13
31	1			..	1	12
32	..			2	2	11
33	1			..	1	9
34	..			..	..	8
35	1			2	3	8
36	1	..		2	3	5
37	..			1	1	2
38				..	1	1
39		..		1	1	1
	308	6	202	74	590	5551

AGE AT ENTRY 44 (Next Birthday)

NUMBER OF ENTRANTS 501

Years of Assurance	Existing	Matured	Withdrawn	Died	Total	Exposed to Risk of Death
	..	..	14	1	14	
1	17	..	68	1	86	487
2	14	..	21	1	36	401
3	17		19	3	39	365
4	18		8	2	28	326
5	16	1	13	5	35	293
6	8	..	9	3	20	263
7	13	..	8	4	25	243
8	10	..	3	3	16	218
9	12	..	4	3	19	202
10	15	..	3	2	20	183
11	6	..	1	3	10	163
12	16	..	2	1	19	153
13	20	..	2	..	22	134
14	11	..	1	2	14	113
15	3	..	1	..	4	98
16	4	3	1	..	8	94
17	3	2	..	1	6	86
18	4	..	..	2	6	80
19	3	..	1	..	4	74
20	7	..	1	1	9	70
21	5	2	..	..	7	61
22	5	..	..	2	7	54
23	10	..	..	2	12	47
24	3	..	..	..	3	35
25	..	..	..	4	4	32
26	3	..	..	..	3	28
27	3	..	..	1	4	25
28	1	..	..	..	1	21
29	2	..		1	3	20
30	..	..		..	..	17
31	3	..	..	1	4	17
32	1	..	..	3	4	13
33	1	..	..	..	1	9
34	1		..	..	1	8
35	..	..	..	3	3	3
36	1	..	..	..	1	4
37		..	..	1	1	3
38		..	..	..	1	2
39		..	..	..	..	1
40		..	..	..	..	1
41	..	..	..	..	..	1
42	1	..	..	..	1	1
	257	8	180	56	501	4457

TABLE I.—Continued.

AGE AT ENTRY 45 (Next Birthday.)

NUMBER OF ENTRANTS 486.

Years of Assurance	Existing	Matured	Withdrawn	Died	Total	Exposed to Risk of Death
	..	..	14	..	14	
1	15	..	51	3	69	472
2	14	..	13	..	27	403
3	17	..	13	2	32	376
4	15	..	7	7	29	344
5	13	..	13	2	28	315
6	12	..	2	2	16	287
7	25	..	6	1	32	271
8	8	..	3	4	15	239
9	8	..	3	2	13	224
10	14	..	6	5	25	211
11	12	..	2	1	15	186
12	11	..	2	6	19	171
13	8	..	2	2	12	152
14	9	..	..	2	11	140
15	7	4	..	5	16	129
16	6	..	..	5	11	113
17	6	..	3	4	13	102
18	5	..	1	5	11	89
19	1	..	..	3	4	78
20	6	..	..	1	7	74
21	8	1	..	..	9	67
22	12	..	..	2	14	58
23	8	..	..	3	11	44
24	6	..	..	2	8	33
25	1	..	..	..	1	25
26	2	..	..	2	4	24
27	2	..	..	2	4	20
28	1	..	..	3	4	16
29	2	..	..	1	3	12
30	..	..	1	..	1	9
31	..	..	..	1	1	8
32	2	..	..	1	3	7
33	1	..	1	..	2	4
34	..	..	..	1	1	2
35	..	..	..	..	..	1
36	..	..	..	..	..	1
37	..	..	..	..	..	1
38	..	..	..	..	..	1
39	..	..	..	1	1	1
	257	5	143	81	486	4710

AGE AT ENTRY 46 (Next Birthday.)

NUMBER OF ENTRANTS 386.

Years of Assurance	Existing	Matured	Withdrawn	Died	Total	Exposed to Risk of Death
	..	..	9	..	9	
1	10	..	43	6	59	377
2	9	1	13	1	24	318
3	15	..	11	1	27	294
4	11	..	6	3	20	267
5	7	..	13	4	24	247
6	9	..	7	2	18	223
7	12	..	8	3	23	205
8	10	..	3	2	15	182
9	5	..	2	4	11	167
10	12	..	5	3	20	156
11	6	..	3	1	10	136
12	11	..	4	..	15	126
13	11	..	..	..	11	111
14	6	..	1	1	8	100
15	6	..	2	2	10	92
16	5	..	..	2	7	82
17	6	..	..	..	6	75
18	5	..	..	..	5	69
19	6	..	2	1	9	64
20	4	..	1	..	5	55
21	13	..	1	1	15	50
22	6	..	..	..	6	35
23	10	..	1	..	11	29
24	2	..	..	1	3	18
25	..	..	..	1	1	15
26	..	..	..	..	..	14
27	2	..	..	1	3	14
28	3	..	..	..	3	11
29	..	..	..	..	..	8
30	..	..	..	..	..	8
31	..	..	..	..	..	8
32	1	..	..	1	2	8
33	1	..	..	..	1	6
34	..	..	..	1	1	5
35	..	..	..	1	1	4
36	1	..	..	..	1	3
37	..	..	..	..	..	2
38	..	..	..	..	..	2
39	1	..	..	..	1	2
40	..	..	..	..	..	1
41	..	..	..	..	..	1
42	..	..	..	..	..	1
43	..	..	..	..	..	1
44	..	..	..	..	..	1
45	..	..	..	1	1	1
	206	1	135	44	386	3594

TABLE I. Continued.

AGE AT ENTRY 47 (New birthday) NUMBER OF ENTRANTS 364

AGE AT ENTRY 48 (New birthday) NUMBER OF ENTRANTS 323

Years of Assurance	Existing	Matured	Withdrawn	Died	Total	Exposed to Risk of Death	Years of Assurance	Existing	Matured	Withdrawn	Died	Total	Exposed to Risk of Death
			8		8					6		6	
1	20	1	30	2	53	336	1	14		30		44	382
2	8		14	3	25	303	2	4		11	2	17	373
3	11		16	3	30	278	3	9		9	3	23	356
4	14		6	1	21	248	4	10		6	2	18	233
5	6		11	2	22	227	5	12		7	2	21	215
6	8		7	1	16	205	6	2		8	5	15	193
7	12		1	2	15	189	7	12		2	4	18	179
8	14		6	4	24	174	8	9		4	2	15	161
9	6			1	7	150	9	9		3		12	146
10	13	1	1	3	18	143	10	11	1	2	2	16	134
11	10		1	4	15	125	11	7		1	1	9	118
12	9		3	1	13	110	12	14	1	2	2	19	109
13	15	1		3	19	97	13	12	1	1	3	17	90
14	5	1	1	2	9	78	14	6		1		7	73
15	5		1	1	7	69	15	5			2	7	66
16	4		1		5	62	16	4			2	6	59
17	3			3	6	57	17	4		1	2	7	53
18	2	1	1	2	6	51	18	4			4	8	46
19	6	1	1	3	10	45	19	3				3	38
20	4		1	2	7	35	20	5			2	7	35
21	3			1	4	28	21	3			1	4	28
22	6			1	7	24	22				2	2	24
23						17	23	3			2	5	22
24	3				3	17	24	1			1	2	17
25						14	25	1			2	3	15
26			1	1	2	14	26			1		1	12
27	1		1	1	3	12	27				1	1	11
28						9	28	1				1	10
29				1	1	9	29				1	1	9
30				1	1	8	30						8
31			1	1	2	7	31						8
32				2	2	5	32	1				1	8
33						3	33				4	4	7
34				1	1	3	34						3
35						2	35						3
36						2	36				1	2	3
37						2	37				1	1	2
38						2	38						1
39						2	39				1	1	1
40						2							
41						2							
42						2							
43	1			1	2	2							
	192	6	112	54	364	3190		166	3	95	59	323	2987

TABLE I. Continued.

AGE AT ENTRY 49 (Next Birthday.)

NUMBER OF ENTRANTS 293

Years of Assurance	Existing	Ma-tured	With-drawn	Died	Total	Exposed to Risk of Death
	..	..	7	.	7	
1	12	..	33	2	47	286
2	8		12	5	25	259
3	11		13	3	27	234
4	7	.	7	1	15	187
5	9	1	4	3	17	172
6	7	.	8	3	18	155
7	3	1	6	2	12	137
8	8		..	2	10	125
9	4	..	3	5	12	115
10	5	3	..	4	12	103
11	4	..	1	3	8	91
12	6	1	..	3	10	83
13	9		..	3	12	73
14	5		1	2	8	61
15	7	..	2	1	10	53
16	5	2	..	3	10	43
17	3	1	..	.	4	33
18	3	..	1	.	4	29
19	1				1	25
20	2			.	2	24
21	.			5	5	22
22	2			..	2	17
23	3				3	15
24	1				1	12
25	2				2	11
26	1				1	9
27					.	6
28						6
29	1			2	3	6
30						3
31				1	1	3
32				1	1	2
33					1	1
34					1	1
35					1	1
36					1	1
37				1	1	1
	131	9	98	55	293	2365

AGE AT ENTRY 50 (Next Birthday.)

NUMBER OF ENTRANTS 283.

Years of Assurance	Existing	Ma-tured	With-drawn	Died	Total	Exposed to Risk of Death
	..	..	7	..	7	
1	14	1	28	2	45	276
2	6	..	18	1	25	231
3	4	..	7	3	14	206
4	11	..	4	..	15	192
5	13	..	7	3	23	177
6	7	..	1	3	11	154
7	5	..	3	2	10	143
8	7	..	2	2	11	133
9	9	..	..	2	11	122
10	13	1	1	3	18	114
11	7	1	1	2	11	93
12	4	..	..	1	5	82
13	6	..	1	2	9	77
14	9	..	..	4	13	68
15	5	1	..	1	8	55
16	2	..	..	1	4	47
17	2	..	2	..	4	43
18	5	..	..	1	6	39
19	5	..	..	4	9	33
20	1	..	1	1	3	24
21	2	..			2	21
22	5				5	19
23	1			2	3	14
24	1				1	11
25					..	10
26				1	1	10
27				2	2	9
28				1	1	7
29				2	2	6
30	1			1	2	1
31						2
32					..	2
33			1	1		2
34						1
35						1
36						1
37						1
38						1
39						1
40						1
41						1
42				1	1	1
	145	4	85	49	283	2432

TABLE I. -Continued.

AGE AT ENTRY 51 (Next Birthday.)

NUMBER OF ENTRANTS 203

Year of Assurance	Existing	Me. geal.	With-drawn	Died	Total	Exposed to Risk of Death
			8		8	
1	11		19	1	31	195
2	6		5		11	164
3	3		2		5	153
4	5		1	2	9	148
5	8		3	1	12	139
6	7		6	3	16	127
7	8		2		11	111
8	5			2	10	100
9	3		2		5	90
10	6	1	2		16	85
11	5			3	8	74
12	6			2	10	66
13	2			3	5	56
14	3		1	1	9	54
15	8			3	8	45
16	3			1	34	
17	4			1	5	33
18	3			1	4	25
19	3				3	24
20	2		1		3	21
21	1				1	12
22	3			1	1	11
23	1			2	3	10
24				1	2	
25				3	3	6
26						2
27						3
28				2	2	5
29						1
30						1
31				1	1	1
	114	1	51	37	203	1808

AGE AT ENTRY 52 (Next Birthday)

NUMBER OF ENTRANTS 175

Year of Assurance	Existing	Me. gened	With-drawn	Died	Total	Exposed to Risk of Death
			9		9	
1	7		25		32	166
2	3		9	3	15	134
3	4		3	1	8	119
4	5		3	2	10	111
5	6		2		8	101
6	1		4	3	8	95
7	5		1	1	7	85
8	3		2		5	78
9	6			2	8	73
10	6		2	2	10	63
11	4		1		5	55
12	3				7	50
13	6	1			7	43
14	3			1	4	39
15	3		4	1	5	32
16	5		1	5	9	27
17	3				3	18
18	2				2	15
19				1	1	13
20						12
21	2			2	1	12
22	3				3	
23	1					1
24						1
25	3			1	4	3
26				1	1	2
27						1
28						1
29						1
30						1
31						1
32						1
33						1
34						1
35						1
36				1	1	1
	84	1	63	27	175	1371

TABLE I.—Continued.

AGE AT ENTRY 53 (Next Birthday.)   AGE AT ENTRY 54 (Next Birthday.)

Years of Assurance	NUMBER OF ENTRANTS 149.						Years of Assurance	NUMBER OF ENTRANTS 113.					
	Existing	Matured	Withdrawn	Died	Total	Exposed to Risk of Death.		Existing	Matured	Withdrawn	Died	Total	Exposed to Risk of Death.
	..	..	6	..	6			..	..	2	..	2	
1	12	..	16	..	28	143	1	7	..	10	..	17	111
2	6	..	5	2	13	115	2	5	..	1	1	7	94
3	2	..	5	2	9	102	3	2	..	2	1	5	87
4	4	..	..	2	6	93	4	7	..	2	..	9	82
5	4	..	3	1	8	87	5	5	..	6	2	13	73
6	4	..	..	4	8	79	6	6	..	3	..	9	60
7	4	..	..	2	6	71	7	3	..	..	1	4	51
8	2	..	1	1	4	65	8	3	..	..	2	5	47
9	1	..	1	1	3	61	9	1	..	..	1	2	42
10	3	..	..	2	5	58	10	2	..	1	..	3	40
11	1	..	1	1	3	53	11	5	..	1	1	7	37
12	2	1	..	1	4	50	12	5	..	..	1	6	30
13	8	..	1	1	10	46	13	5	..	..	..	5	24
14	3	..	3	2	8	36	14	..	..	..	..	..	19
15	1	..	1	1	3	28	15	4	..	..	..	4	19
16	1	..	1	..	2	25	16	..	..	..	1	1	15
17	3	..	..	..	3	23	17	..	..	..	2	2	14
18	..	..	..	..	..	20	18	..	..	..	..	..	12
19	1	..	1	..	2	20	19	2	..	..	..	2	12
20	2	..	..	2	4	18	20	1	..	..	..	1	10
21	2	..	1	1	4	14	21	..	..	..	1	1	9
22	1	..	..	1	2	10	22	..	..	..	..	..	8
23	3	..	..	1	4	8	23	1	..	..	1	2	8
24	..	..	..	..	..	4	24	..	..	..	..	..	6
25	..	..	..	2	2	4	25	..	..	..	..	..	6
26	..	..	..	..	..	2	26	1	..	..	..	1	6
27	..	..	..	..	..	2	27	..	..	1	2	3	5
28	..	..	..	..	..	2	28	..	..	..	..	..	2
29	..	..	..	..	..	2	29	..	..	..	..	..	2
30	1	..	..	1	2	2	30	..	..	..	1	1	2
							31	..	..	..	..	..	1
							32	..	..	..	..	..	1
							33	..	..	..	..	..	1
							34	..	..	..	1	1	1
	71	1	46	31	149	1243		65	0	29	19	113	937

TABLE I. Continued.

AGE AT ENTRY 55 (Next Birthday)

NUMBER OF ENTRANTS 131

Years of Assurance	Existing	Matured	Withdrawn	Died	Total	Exposed to Risk of Death
	.	..	2		2	
1	9	..	10	..	19	159
2	3	1	6	1	11	110
3	7		5	1	13	99
4	11	..	-	1	12	86
5	7	1	1	2	11	74
6	3	..	1	4	8	63
7	5	..			5	55
8	3		4	4	11	50
9	3	..			3	39
10	4	1	3	1	9	36
11	3		1		4	27
12	3		1	2	6	23
13	2			2	4	17
14				1	1	13
15				1	1	12
16	1		1		2	11
17				2	2	9
18	1			1		7
19				1	1	6
20						5
21						5
22				1	1	5
23						4
24	1			2	3	4
25						2
26						1
27						1
28				1	1	1
	66	3	35	27	131	893

AGE AT ENTRY 56 (Next Birthday)

NUMBER OF ENTRANTS 80.

Years of Assurance	Existing	Matured	Withdrawn	Died	Total	Exposed to Risk of Death
	.		1	..	1	
1	2	..	8	1	11	79
2	4		3	1	8	68
3	3	..	3	1	7	60
4	3	..	..	..	3	53
5	2	..	1	1	4	50
6	1	..	1	1	3	46
7	3	..			3	43
8	6			1	7	40
9			1	2	3	33
10	2			1	3	30
11	2			2	4	27
12	2				2	23
13	2				2	21
14	3				2	19
15	2				2	17
16	2			4	6	13
17	1			..	1	9
18	1			1	2	5
19				1	1	6
20	1			1	2	5
21	1					3
22	1			1	1	2
23	1				1	1
	44	0	18	18	80	658

TABLE I. Continued.

AGE AT ENTRY 57 (Next Birthday.)

NUMBER OF ENTRANTS 74

Years of Assurance	Existing.	Matured.	With-drawn.	Died.	Total.	Exposed to Risk of Death.
			1		1	
1	6	..	7		13	73
2	5		2		5	60
3	3		2	2	7	55
4	3		..		3	48
5	2		2	1	5	45
6	1		..		1	40
7			1	..	2	39
8	3		..	1	4	37
9	1		..		1	33
10	1	..	3	1	5	32
11	3		..	..	3	27
12	1		..	2	3	24
13	1		1		2	21
14	1			2	3	19
15						16
16	1			3	4	16
17	1				1	12
18	3	..	..	..	3	11
19						8
20	2		1	1	4	8
21	1				1	4
22	1			1	2	3
23						1
24						1
25						1
26				1	1	1
	39	0	20	15	74	635

AGE AT ENTRY 58 (Next Birthday.)

NUMBER OF ENTRANTS 61.

Years of Assurance	Existing.	Matured.	With-drawn.	Died.	Total.	Exposed to Risk of Death.
			1	..	1	
1	5	..	6	1	12	60
2	3	..	1	1	5	48
3		..	1		1	43
4	1	..	..	1	2	42
5	2	..	1	..	3	40
6	4				4	37
7	2				2	33
8	4	..	..	2	6	31
9	1		..	2	3	25
10	3	..	..	2	5	22
11	1		1	1	3	17
12	1		..		1	14
13						13
14	2				2	13
15	1			1	2	11
16	1				1	9
17	1	..		3	4	8
18		..				4
19						4
20	2	..			2	4
21	1				1	2
22						1
23						1
24						1
25						1
26						1
27				1	1	1
	35	0	11	15	61	486

TABLE I.—Continued.

AGE AT ENTRY 59 (Next Birthday)

NUMBER OF ENTRANTS 53

Years of Assurance	Existing	Ma-tured	With-drawn	Died	Total	Exposed to Risk of Death
			2		2	
1	4		7		11	51
2	3		3	3	9	40
3	2		1		3	31
4	2		2	1	5	28
5	1		..	1	2	23
6			..	..	..	21
7	1	..	1	..	2	21
8	2	..		1	3	19
9	1			1	1	16
10	..	..			..	15
11	2		..	2	4	15
12		..	..		..	11
13	1		1	1	3	11
14	1			1	2	8
15	..			1	1	6
16	1				1	5
17						4
18						4
19				1	1	4
20	1			1	2	3
21	..					1
22						1
23						1
24			1	1		1
	22	0	17	14	53	340

AGE AT ENTRY 60 (Next Birthday)

NUMBER OF ENTRANTS 46

Years of Assurance	Existing	Ma-tured	With-drawn	Died	Total	Exposed to Risk of Death
			6			
1	3		6		9	46
2	4		2		6	37
3	1			1	2	31
4	3			1	4	29
5	1		3	1	5	25
6			..			20
7	1				1	20
8	2		1	1	4	19
9						15
10	1	..	..		1	15
11	2		1		3	14
12	2				2	11
13	2	..		1	3	9
14	..		3		3	6
15	...			1		3
16	1			1	2	3
17						2
18						1
19						1
20				1	1	1
	23	0	13	10	46	307

TABLE I. Continued.

AGE AT ENTRY 61 (Next Birthday.)   AGE AT ENTRY 62 (Next Birthday.)

Years of Assurance	NUMBER OF ENTRANTS 21.						Years of Assurance	NUMBER OF ENTRANTS 18.					
	Lapsing	Matured	With-drawn	Died	Total	Exposed to Risk of Death		Existing	Matured	With-drawn	Died	Total	Exposed to Risk of Death
	..	..	..	..	..			..		1		1	
1	..	1	2	..	3	21	1	2		2		4	17
2	1	..	1	1	3	18	2	..		..	1	1	13
3			..	..		15	3	..	..	..	..	..	12
4		..	..	..		15	4	..		..	1	1	12
5		..	..	1	1	15	5	..		2	..	2	11
6		..	1	..	1	14	6	1	..	..	2	3	9
7	1	..	1		2	13	7	..	..	..	..		6
8		..	1		1	11	8	..	..				6
9	1	..	..		1	10	9	..	..		..		6
10		..	1		1	9	10	..	..		1	1	6
11	1	..	..		1	8	11	2	..		..	2	5
12	1	..	..		1	7	12	2	..			2	3
13	1	..	..		1	6	13	..	..				1
14	1	..		.	1	5	14	..	..		1		1
15	..	..		..		4	15				1		1
16		..		1	1	4	16		..				1
17				..		3	17						1
18		..		..	..	3	18			1			1
19	..	..		1	1	3	19					..	1
20	1			.	1	2	20				1	1	1
21		..				1							
22		..				1							
23						1							
24						1							
25		..		..		1							
26		..				1							
27		..		..		1							
28						1							
29				..		1							
30						1							
31						1							
32						1							
33						1							
34						1							
35						1							
36						1							
37	..			1	1	1							
	8	1	7	5	21	203		8	0	5	5	18	114

TABLE I. Continued.

AGE AT ENTRY 63 (Next Birthday)

NUMBER OF ENTRANTS 14.

Years of Assurance	Existing	Matured	Withdrawn	Died	Total	Exposed to Risk of Death
	..		..		1	
1	2		1		3	13
2	..		1	..	..	10
3	..			1	1	10
4	..			..	..	9
5	2				2	9
6	1			1	2	7
7	1				1	5
8	1				1	4
9						3
10				..		3
11			1	1	1	3
12			1		1	2
13						1
14						1
15						1
16						1
17						1
18						1
19						1
20						1
21						1
22						1
23						1
24			1	1	1	1
	7	0	2	5	14	90

AGE AT ENTRY 64 (Next Birthday)

NUMBER OF ENTRANTS 18.

Years of Assurance	Existing	Matured	Withdrawn	Died	Total	Exposed to Risk of Death
	..		..	..		
1	3	..	2	1	6	18
2	1	..	..	..	1	12
3	2	...	..		2	11
4	4		..		4	9
5	1		..		1	5
6	2			..	2	4
7	1			1	2	2
	14	0	2	2	18	61

TABLE I. Continued.

AGE AT ENTRY 65 (Next Birthday.)

Years of Assurance	NUMBER OF ENTRANTS 20.					
	Existing	Matured	Withdrawn	Died	Total	Exposed to Risk of Death.
1	1	..	..	1	2	20
2	..	..	1	1	2	18
3	..	..	2	..	2	16
4	2	..	..	..	2	14
5	1	..	1	..	2	12
6	1	..	..	..	1	10
7	1	..	..	1	2	9
8	..	..	..	..	..	7
9	1	..	..	1	2	7
10				1	1	5
11					..	4
12			3		3	4
13						1
14						1
15						1
16						1
17	1				1	1
	8	0	4	8	20	131

AGE AT ENTRY 66 (Next Birthday.)

Years of Assurance	NUMBER OF ENTRANTS 8.					
	Existing	Matured	Withdrawn	Died	Total	Exposed to Risk of Death.
1	1	..	1	..	2	8
2	..	..	..	..	..	6
3	1	..	..	..	1	6
4	..	..	..	1	1	5
5	..	..	..	..	..	4
6	1	..	..	..	1	4
7					..	3
8	..	..	1	..	1	3
9					..	2
10			..		..	2
11			..		..	2
12	..	..	1	..	1	2
13				1	1	1
	3	0	3	2	8	48

TABLE I.—Continued.

AGE AT ENTRY 67 (Next Birthday.)   AGE AT ENTRY 68 (Next Birthday.)

Years of Assurance	NUMBER OF ENTRANTS 5						Years of Assurance	NUMBER OF ENTRANTS 5					
	Existing	Matured	With-drawn	Died	Total	Exposed to Risk of Death		Existing	Matured	With-drawn	Died	Total	Exposed to Risk of Death
			1		1							. .	
1	. .		. .			1	1					. .	5
2	1		1		2	1	2	. .		1		1	5
3						2	3	1				1	4
4			1	1		2	4						5
5						1	5	. .			1	1	3
6						1	6	1				1	2
7	1			1		1	7						1
							8						1
							9						1
							10						1
							11						1
							12				1	1	1
	2	0	2	1	5	15		2	0	1	2	5	28

TABLE 1.—Continued.

AGE AT ENTRY 69 (Next Birthday.)

Years of Assurance	NUMBER OF ENTRANTS 1.					
	Existing.	Matured.	Withdrawn.	Died.	Total.	Exposed to Risk of Death.
1	..	..	..	..	..	1
2	..	..	..	..	..	1
3	..	..	..	..	..	1
4	..	..	..	..	..	1
5	..	..	..	..	..	1
6	..	..	..	..	..	1
7		..	..	1	1	1
	0	0	0	1	1	7

AGE AT ENTRY 70 (Next Birthday.)

Years of Assurance	NUMBER OF ENTRANTS 0.					
	Existing.	Matured.	Withdrawn.	Died.	Total.	Exposed to Risk of Death.

AGE AT ENTRY 71 (Next Birthday.)

Years of Assurance	NUMBER OF ENTRANTS 1.					
	Existing.	Matured.	Withdrawn.	Died.	Total.	Exposed to Risk of Death.
1			..	1	1	1
	0	0	0	1	1	1

TABLE II.

SUMMARY OF OBSERVATIONS.

Age at Entry (Next Birthday)	Number of Entrants	Ultimate Disposal of Entrants				Age of Entry (Next Birthday)	Number of Entrants	Ultimate Disposal of Entrants			
		Dead	Matured and Withdrawn	Withdrawn within first six months	Existing			Dead	Matured and Withdrawn	Withdrawn within first six months	Existing
15	5		4		1	45	486	81	131	13	257
16	14	1	5	..	8	46	386	44	127	9	206
17	37	2	10	..	25	47	364	54	110	8	162
18	92	6	24	2	60	48	323	59	92	6	166
19	227	8	51	11	157	49	293	55	100	7	131
20	504	17	136	23	328	50	283	49	82	7	145
21	1503	75	486	47	895	51	203	37	44	8	114
22	1508	69	515	68	856	52	175	27	55	9	84
23	1708	83	583	72	970	53	149	31	41	6	71
24	1725	93	593	66	973	54	113	19	27	2	65
25	1765	80	607	67	1011	55	131	27	36	2	66
26	1730	92	637	55	946	56	80	18	17	1	44
27	1762	88	608	75	991	57	74	15	19	1	39
28	1738	105	585	63	985	58	61	15	10	1	35
29	1645	113	542	57	943	59	53	14	15	2	22
30	1587	108	557	50	872	60	46	10	13	..	23
31	1619	95	575	64	885	61	21	5	8	..	8
32	1516	105	524	63	824	62	18	5	4	1	8
33	1378	114	507	50	707	63	14	5	1	1	7
34	1278	118	453	40	667	64	18	2	2		14
35	1231	101	440	41	649	65	20	8	4		8
36	1145	97	397	46	605	66	8	2	3	..	3
37	1077	95	366	33	583	67	5	1	1	1	2
38	990	82	337	40	431	68	5	2	1		2
39	860	95	268	27	470	69	1	1		..	
40	815	76	253	23	463	70	..	..			
41	742	82	256	19	385	71	1	1			
42	636	72	206	24	354						
43	590	74	193	15	368						
44	504	56	172	14	252	Total	35287	2789	11838	1241	19419

TABLE III.

Part 1.—Unadjusted Exposures and Deaths for ages to be attained next birthday.

Part 2. Exposures and Deaths for completed ages, with radix of 10,000 at age 20. Unadjusted.

PART 1.

Age next Birthday	Exposed E_{x+1}	Died d_{x+1}	Age next Birthday	Exposed E_{x+1}	Died d_{x+1}
15	5	..	57	3,541	54
16	19	..	58	3,023	54
17	52	..	59	2,740	65
18	126	..	60	2,378	61
19	318	1	61	2,094	50
20	726	5	62	1,861	52
21	2,026	4	63	1,655	54
22	3,075	19	64	1,461	35
23	4,181	18	65	1,282	41
24	5,151	25	66	1,120	40
25	6,042	36	67	953	36
26	6,809	42	68	827	33
27	7,513	31	69	692	31
28	8,215	36	70	600	25
29	8,785	42	71	519	25
30	9,274	51	72	435	33
31	9,736	48	73	359	23
32	10,068	46	74	287	20
33	10,287	53	75	239	20
34	10,446	72	76	196	14
35	10,530	63	77	163	14
36	10,500	75	78	121	19
37	10,421	56	79	89	12
38	10,244	61	80	65	11
39	10,015	62	81	48	7
40	9,802	82	82	33	6
41	9,534	68	83	22	5
42	9,201	49	84	16	3
43	8,864	64	85	12	1
44	8,425	64	86	9	2
45	8,002	65	87	7	2
46	7,602	64	88	5	..
47	7,198	75	89	5	1
48	6,800	70	90	3	1
49	6,378	58	91	2	1
50	5,992	61	92	1	..
51	5,553	66	93	1	..
52	5,134	55	94	1	..
53	4,751	60	95	1	..
54	4,358	74	96	1	..
55	4,002	58	97	1	1
56	3,665	39	TOTAL.	296,481	2,789

PART 2.

Completed Age x	Exposed E_x	Died d_x	Completed Age x	Exposed E_x	Died d_x
20	10,000	51	60	7,064	177
21	9,947	33	61	6,887	174
22	9,914	55	62	6,713	198
23	9,859	44	63	6,515	194
24	9,815	52	64	6,321	168
25	9,763	58	65	6,153	204
26	9,705	54	66	5,949	217
27	9,651	43	67	5,732	220
28	9,608	43	68	5,512	229
29	9,565	48	69	5,283	231
30	9,517	51	70	5,052	221
31	9,466	45	71	4,831	276
32	9,421	45	72	4,555	333
33	9,376	54	73	4,222	274
34	9,322	61	74	3,948	295
35	9,261	59	75	3,653	291
36	9,202	61	76	3,362	256
37	9,141	51	77	3,108	333
38	9,090	54	78	2,775	410
39	9,036	63	79	2,365	343
40	8,973	71	80	2,022	328
41	8,902	58	81	1,691	266
42	8,844	53	82	1,423	278
43	8,791	65	83	1,150	249
44	8,726	67	84	901	142
45	8,659	72	85	759	96
46	8,587	78	86	663	159
47	8,509	88	87	504	106
48	8,421	83	88	398	27
49	8,338	79	89	371	88
50	8,259	89	90	283	106
51	8,170	94	91	177	71
52	8,076	91	92	106	..
53	7,985	113	93	106	..
54	7,872	127	94	106	..
55	7,745	114	95	106	..
56	7,631	119	96	106	35
57	7,512	126	97	71	71
58	7,386	146			
59	7,240	176			

TABLE IV.

GRADUATED MORTALITY TABLE.

GENERAL EXPERIENCE.

Age.	Number Living. l_x	Number Dying. d_x	Probability of Living a Year. p_x	Probability of Dying in a Year. q_x	Complete Expectation of Life. e_x
20	100,000	463	.995373	.004627	46.219
21	99,537	464	.995335	.004665	45.462
22	99,073	466	.995294	.004706	44.673
23	98,607	469	.995248	.004752	43.881
24	98,138	471	.995197	.004803	43.089
25	97,667	475	.995142	.004858	42.294
26	97,192	478	.995080	.004920	41.498
27	96,714	482	.995013	.004987	40.701
28	96,232	487	.994938	.005062	39.902
29	95,745	493	.994856	.005144	39.103
30	95,252	499	.994765	.005235	38.303
31	94,753	505	.994665	.005335	37.502
32	94,248	513	.994555	.005445	36.700
33	93,735	522	.994433	.005567	35.898
34	93,213	532	.994298	.005702	35.096
35	92,681	542	.994150	.005850	34.298
36	92,139	554	.993987	.006013	33.491
37	91,585	567	.993807	.006193	32.693
38	91,018	582	.993609	.006391	31.894
39	90,436	597	.993390	.006610	31.096
40	89,839	616	.993148	.006852	30.299
41	89,223	635	.992882	.007118	29.505
42	88,588	657	.992590	.007410	28.713
43	87,931	680	.992265	.007735	27.924
44	87,251	706	.991909	.008091	27.137
45	86,545	734	.991516	.008484	26.355
46	85,811	765	.991082	.008918	25.576
47	85,046	799	.990604	.009396	24.801
48	84,247	836	.990078	.009922	24.032
49	83,411	876	.989497	.010503	23.268
50	82,535	920	.988857	.011143	22.509
51	81,615	967	.988151	.011849	21.757
52	80,648	1,018	.987374	.012626	21.012
53	79,630	1,074	.986518	.013482	20.275
54	78,556	1,133	.985574	.014426	19.545
55	77,423	1,198	.984534	.015466	18.824
56	76,225	1,266	.983388	.016612	18.112
57	74,959	1,340	.982126	.017874	17.409
58	73,619	1,418	.980736	.019264	16.717
59	72,201	1,501	.979208	.020792	16.035
60	70,700	1,590	.977520	.022480	15.365
61	69,110	1,682	.975664	.024336	14.707
62	67,428	1,778	.973622	.026378	14.061

TABLE IV.—Continued.

GRADUATED MORTALITY TABLE.

GENERAL EXPERIENCE.

Age.	Number Living. l_x	Number Dying. d_x	Probability of Living a Year. p_x	Probability of Dying in a Year. q_x	Complete Expectation of Life. $\overset{\circ}{e}_x$
63	65,650	1,880	.971374	.028626	13.429
64	63,770	1,983	.968901	.031099	12.810
65	61,787	2,089	.966181	.033819	12.205
66	59,698	2,198	.963189	.036811	11.615
67	57,500	2,306	.959901	.040099	11.039
68	55,194	2,412	.956287	.043713	10.480
69	52,782	2,517	.952318	.047682	9.936
70	50,265	2,616	.947959	.052041	9.408
71	47,649	2,707	.943175	.056825	8.897
72	44,942	2,790	.937926	.062074	8.403
73	42,152	2,859	.932172	.067828	7.926
74	39,293	2,913	.925866	.074134	7.467
75	36,380	2,948	.918959	.081041	7.025
76	33,432	2,962	.911402	.088598	6.600
77	30,470	2,952	.903140	.096860	6.193
78	27,518	2,913	.894115	.105885	5.804
79	24,605	2,848	.884266	.115734	5.431
80	21,757	2,752	.873529	.126471	5.077
81	19,005	2,625	.861839	.138161	4.740
82	16,380	2,472	.849127	.150873	4.419
83	13,908	2,290	.835324	.164676	4.116
84	11,618	2,087	.820362	.179638	3.828
85	9,531	1,867	.804170	.195830	3.557
86	7,664	1,634	.786682	.213318	3.302
87	6,030	1,400	.767835	.232165	3.061
88	4,630	1,169	.747573	.252427	2.836
89	3,461	949	.725845	.274155	2.625
90	2,512	747	.702613	.297387	2.427
91	1,765	569	.677852	.322148	2.243
92	1,196	416	.651554	.348446	2.072
93	780	294	.623731	.376269	1.910
94	486	197	.594421	.405579	1.763
95	289	126	.563690	.436310	1.625
96	163	76	.531635	.468365	1.494
97	87	44	.498392	.501608	1.362
98	43	23	.464134	.535866	1.244
99	20	12	.429075	.570925	1.100
100	8	5	.393471	.606529	1.000
101	3	2	.357620	.642380	.833
102	1	1	.000000	1.000000	.500

TABLE V.

Exposures and Deaths at integral ages attained.

On the basis of three times the exposed and died.

Age Attained.	Three Times Number Exposed.	Three Times Number Died.	Age Attained.	Three Times Number Exposed.	Three Times Number Died.
19	1,362	7	60	7,632	172
20	3,478	11	61	6,935	162
21	7,117	22	62	5,573	153
22	10,531	50	63	4,771	143
23	13,513	61	64	3,840	111
24	16,344	86	60-64	27,751	726
20-24	50,793	244	65	3,684	122
25	18,893	113	66	3,393	119
26	21,133	116	67	2,733	105
27	23,218	104	68	2,546	97
28	25,215	111	69	1,984	87
29	26,844	155	65-69	13,940	577
25-29	115,330	582	70	1,716	75
30	28,284	130	71	1,473	83
31	29,540	142	72	1,229	79
32	30,423	145	73	1,025	69
33	31,020	178	74	813	60
34	31,422	207	70-74	6,239	373
30-34	150,689	822	75	674	54
35	31,360	201	76	555	42
36	31,404	206	77	450	47
37	31,052	175	78	337	50
38	30,503	184	79	243	35
39	29,832	206	75-79	2,250	228
35-39	154,351	972	80	173	26
40	29,138	232	81	129	20
41	28,269	185	82	88	17
42	27,265	162	83	62	13
43	26,153	192	84	43	7
44	24,853	193	80-84	490	83
40-44	135,678	964	85	33	3
45	23,620	194	86	23	6
46	22,592	205	87	16	3
47	21,196	220	88	15	1
48	19,978	198	89	13	2
49	18,718	177	85-89	105	13
45-49	105,930	902	90	5	3
50	17,637	188	91	5	2
51	16,140	187	92	4	0
52	15,019	170	93	4	0
53	13,860	194	94	5	0
54	12,718	206	90-94	23	5
50-54	75,371	945	95	3	1
55	11,160	172	96	3	1
56	10,171	186	97	2	1
57	9,705	162	95-97	8	3
58	5,386	151			
59	7,855	193			
55-59	45,684	864	Total.	888,519	8,300

TABLE VI.

Mortality Experience, excluding the first five years of Assurance.

Age x	Exposed $E_{x-\frac{1}{2}}$	Died $d_{x-\frac{1}{2}}$	Adjusted Annual Rates of Mortality. q_x	Age x	Exposed $E_{x-\frac{1}{2}}$	Died $d_{x-\frac{1}{2}}$	Adjusted Annual Rates of Mortality. q_x
25	282	..	.00639	50	4,726	44	.01174
26	913	8	.00641	51	4,453	57	.01243
27	1,433	9	.00644	52	4,196	49	.01319
28	2,061	11	.00648	53	3,957	54	.01404
29	2,658	19	.00652	54	3,688	66	.01498
30	3,243	25	.00657	55	3,427	52	.01602
31	3,729	19	.00662	56	3,195	51	.01716
32	4,251	26	.00668	57	2,932	51	.01843
33	5,775	30	.00674	58	2,684	49	.01983
34	5,176	45	.00681	59	2,459	60	.02137
35	5,510	42	.00690	60	2,151	57	.02307
36	5,752	41	.00701	61	1,918	48	.02492
37	5,963	35	.00715	62	1,727	49	.02695
38	6,071	41	.00731	63	1,562	51	.02918
39	6,168	44	.00749	64	1,381	33	.03162
40	6,276	63	.00770	65	1,213	38	.03430
41	6,240	52	.00794	66	1,063	39	.03725
42	6,214	30	.00820	67	909	36	.04049
43	6,163	49	.00839	68	793	33	.04405
44	6,010	56	.00882	69	667	30	.04795
45	5,843	54	.00919	70	589	24	.05223
46	5,681	50	.00960	71	513	24	.05694
47	5,162	65	.01006	72	431	32	.06213
48	5,244	54	.01056	73	358	23	.06784
49	4,939	46	.01112	74	287	20	.07413

TABLE VII.

SELECT TABLE.

Annual Rates of Mortality for different ages at entry and different periods since entry.

Age	0	1	2	3	4	5 or More	Age	5 or More
	$q_{[x]}$	$q_{[x-1]+1}$	$q_{[x-2]+2}$	$q_{[x-3]+3}$	$q_{[x-4]+4}$	$q_{x(5)}$		$q_{x(5)}$
20	.00237	..					55	.01602
21	.00238	.00379	..				56	.01716
22	.00240	.00383	.00403	..			57	.01843
23	.00243	.00386	.00397	.00573	..		58	.01983
24	.00246	.00389	.00500	.00576	.00620		59	.02137
25	.00250	.00393	.00503	.00579	.00622	.00639	60	.02307
26	.00255	.00397	.00507	.00582	.00625	.00641	61	.02492
27	.00261	.00402	.00511	.00586	.00628	.00644	62	.02695
28	.00267	.00407	.00516	.00590	.00632	.00648	63	.02918
29	.00273	.00413	.00521	.00595	.00637	.00652	64	.03162
30	.00281	.00420	.00527	.00600	.00642	.00657	65	.03430
31	.00289	.00428	.00534	.00606	.00647	.00662	66	.03725
32	.00298	.00436	.00541	.00613	.00653	.00668	67	.04049
33	.00307	.00444	.00548	.00620	.00659	.00674	68	.04405
34	.00317	.00452	.00557	.00628	.00666	.00681	69	.04795
35	.00328	.00461	.00566	.00637	.00675	.00690	70	.05223
36	.00340	.00471	.00577	.00648	.00687	.00701	71	.05694
37	.00352	.00482	.00588	.00661	.00701	.00715	72	.06213
38	.00365	.00493	.00601	.00676	.00716	.00731	73	.06784
39	.00378	.00505	.00615	.00692	.00734	.00749	74	.07413
40	.00392	.00518	.00630	.00710	.00754	.00770		
41	.00407	.00532	.00647	.00730	.00777	.00794		
42	.00423	.00547	.00666	.00753	.00802	.00820		
43	.00439	.00563	.00687	.00778	.00830	.00849		
44	.00456	.00580	.00710	.00807	.00862	.00882		
45	.00473	.00599	.00735	.00839	.00898	.00919		
46	.00492	.00620	.00762	.00874	.00938	.00960		
47	.00511	.00643	.00793	.00912	.00981	.01006		
48	.00531	.00667	.00827	.00954	.01029	.01056		
49	.00551	.00693	.00864	.01001	.01082	.01112		
50	.00573	.00721	.00925	.01053	.01141	.01174		
51	..	.00750	.00950	.01111	.01207	.01243		
52	..	.	.00990	.01175	.01280	.01319		
53				.01246	.01361	.01404		
54	..		..	..	.01451	.01498		

TABLE VIII.

SELECT TABLE.

Values of l_x for different ages at entry and different periods since entry.

Age x	\multicolumn{6}{Years elapsed since date of entry}						Age x	5 or More
	0 $l_{[x]}$	1 $l_{[x-1]+1}$	2 $l_{[x-2]+2}$	3 $l_{[x-3]+3}$	4 $l_{[x-4]+4}$	5 or More $l_{x(5)}$	x	$l_{x(5)}$
20	103,679						55	78,055
21	103,031	103,433					56	76,805
22	102,385	102,786	103,041				57	75,487
23	101,741	102,139	102,392	102,533			58	74,096
24	101,101	101,494	101,745	101,883	101,946		59	72,626
25	100,463	100,853	101,099	101,236	101,296	101,314	60	71,074
26	99,828	100,212	100,456	100,590	100,650	101,666	61	69,435
27	99,193	99,574	99,814	99,947	100,005	100,021	62	67,704
28	98,560	98,934	99,173	99,304	99,361	99,377	63	65,880
29	97,928	98,297	98,532	98,662	98,713	98,733	64	63,957
30	97,298	97,661	97,891	98,018	98,074	98,089	65	61,935
31	96,665	97,024	97,251	97,375	97,430	97,445	66	59,811
32	96,033	96,386	96,609	96,732	96,785	96,800	67	57,583
33	95,395	95,747	95,966	96,086	96,139	96,153	68	55,251
34	94,753	95,102	95,322	95,440	95,491	95,505	69	52,817
35	94,105	94,453	94,672	94,791	94,840	94,855	70	50,285
36	93,448	93,796	94,017	94,137	94,187	94,200	71	47,658
37	92,779	93,130	93,354	93,475	93,527	93,540	72	44,945
38	92,097	92,452	92,681	92,806	92,857	92,871	73	42,152
39	91,401	91,761	91,996	92,124	92,178	92,192	74	39,295
40	90,690	91,056	91,297	91,431	91,487	91,502	75	36,380
41	89,962	90,335	90,584	90,722	90,781	90,797		
42	89,212	89,596	89,854	89,998	90,060	90,076		
43	88,436	88,835	89,105	89,256	89,320	89,337		
44	87,633	88,048	88,335	88,493	88,561	88,579		
45	86,802	87,234	87,537	87,707	87,779	87,798		
46	86,052	86,391	86,711	86,893	86,972	86,991		
47	85,013	85,332	85,855	86,051	86,134	86,156		
48	84,106	84,608	84,883	85,175	85,266	85,289		
49	83,125	83,659	84,044	84,266	84,363	84,388		
50	82,094	82,667	83,080	83,318	83,422	83,450		
51	..	81,626	82,071	82,328	82,440	82,470		
52	..	..	81,013	81,291	81,413	81,445		
53	..	..	..	80,204	80,336	80,371		
54	..	..	..	..	79,205	79,242		

TABLE IX.

GRADUATED MORTALITY TABLE

Excluding the first five years of Assurance.

CANADA LIFE EXPERIENCE

Age.	Number Living. l_x	Number Dying. d_x	Probability of Dying in a Year. q_x	Complete Expectation of Life. e_x	Age.	Number Living. l_x	Number Dying. d_x	Probability of Dying in a Year. q_x	Complete Expectation of Life. e_x
25	101,314	648	.00639	41.352	65	61,935	2,124	.03430	12.182
26	100,666	645	.00641	40.615	66	59,811	2,228	.03725	11.597
27	100,021	644	.00644	39.874	67	57,583	2,332	.04049	11.026
28	99,377	644	.00648	39.129	68	55,251	2,434	.04405	10.471
29	98,733	644	.00652	38.381	69	52,817	2,532	.04795	9.930
30	98,089	644	.00657	37.630	70	50,285	2,627	.05223	9.405
31	97,445	645	.00662	36.875	71	47,658	2,713	.05694	8.896
32	96,800	647	.00668	36.118	72	44,945	2,793	.06213	8.403
33	96,153	648	.00674	35.357	73	42,152	2,859	.06784	7.926
34	95,505	650	.00681	34.594	74	39,293	2,913	.07413	7.467
35	94,855	655	.00690	33.828	75	36,380	2,948	.08104	7.025
36	94,200	660	.00701	33.059	76	33,432	2,962	.08860	6.600
37	93,540	669	.00715	32.289	77	30,470	2,952	.09686	6.193
38	92,871	679	.00731	31.518	78	27,518	2,913	.10589	5.804
39	92,192	690	.00749	30.746	79	24,605	2,848	.11573	5.431
40	91,502	705	.00770	29.975	80	21,757	2,752	.12647	5.077
41	90,797	721	.00794	29.205	81	19,005	2,625	.13816	4.740
42	90,076	739	.00820	28.433	82	16,380	2,472	.15087	4.419
43	89,337	758	.00849	27.664	83	13,908	2,290	.16468	4.119
44	88,579	781	.00882	26.897	84	11,618	2,087	.17964	3.828
45	87,798	807	.00919	26.131	85	9,531	1,867	.19583	3.557
46	86,991	835	.00960	25.369	86	7,664	1,634	.21332	3.302
47	86,156	867	.01006	24.610	87	6,030	1,410	.23217	3.061
48	85,289	901	.01056	23.855	88	4,630	1,169	.25243	2.836
49	84,388	938	.01112	23.105	89	3,461	949	.27416	2.625
50	83,450	980	.01174	22.359	90	2,512	747	.29739	2.427
51	82,470	1,025	.01243	21.619	91	1,765	560	.32215	2.243
52	81,445	1,074	.01319	20.884	92	1,156	416	.34845	2.072
53	80,371	1,129	.01404	20.157	93	780	294	.37627	1.910
54	79,242	1,187	.01495	19.437	94	486	197	.46538	1.763
55	78,055	1,250	.01602	18.725	95	289	126	.43631	1.625
56	76,805	1,318	.01716	18.021	96	163	76	.41837	1.493
57	75,487	1,391	.01843	17.327	97	87	44	.50161	1.302
58	74,096	1,470	.01983	16.643	98	43	23	.53587	1.041
59	72,626	1,552	.02137	15.970	99	20	12	.57503	1.000
60	71,074	1,639	.02307	15.308	100	8	5	.61253	1.000
61	69,435	1,731	.02492	14.657	101	3	2	.63755	.833
62	67,704	1,824	.02695	14.019	102	1	1	1.00000	.500
63	65,880	1,923	.02918	13.394					
64	63,957	2,022	.03162	12.781					

TABLE X.

Annual Rate of Mortality, excluding the first five years of Assurance.

GRADUATED RESULTS.

Age	Canada Life. $q \cdot (5)$	Mutual Life of New York. $q \cdot (5)$	H^m Table. $q \cdot (5)$	Age	Canada Life $q \cdot (5)$	Mutual Life of New York. $q \cdot (5)$	H^m Table. $q \cdot (5)$
25	.006396	.008258	.010506	55	.016014	.015508	.022187
26	.006407	.008282	.010064	56	.017160	.016479	.023506
27	.006439	.008315	.009943	57	.018437	.017575	.025075
28	.006480	.008341	.009704	58	.019839	.018814	.026577
29	.006523	.008376	.009458	59	.021370	.020214	.028360
30	.006565	.008416	.009203	60	.023060	.021794	.030638
31	.006619	.008560	.009172	61	.024930	.023578	.032916
32	.006684	.008512	.009257	62	.026941	.025592	.035583
33	.006739	.008569	.009223	63	.029189	.027866	.038500
34	.006806	.008634	.009223	64	.031615	.030431	.041710
35	.006903	.008708	.010002	65	.034294	.033323	.044614
36	.007006	.008791	.010347	66	.037251	.036585	.047836
37	.007152	.008885	.010701	67	.040498	.040261	.050957
38	.007311	.008992	.011065	68	.044054	.044401	.054449
39	.007484	.009112	.011189	69	.047939	.049063	.058118
40	.007705	.009248	.011316	70	.052242	.054309	.062836
41	.007911	.009402	.011317	71	.056926	.060207	.068539
42	.008204	.009577	.011576	72	.062143	.066834	.075551
43	.008483	.009773	.011844	73	.067826	.074273	.083480
44	.008817	.009996	.012252	74	.074135	.082616	.092231
45	.009192	.010248	.012943	75	.081041	.091961	.099494
46	.009599	.010533	.013659	76	.088598	.102417	.108146
47	.010063	.010855	.014402	77	.096860	.114098	.115486
48	.010561	.011219	.015315	78	.105885	.127128	.124629
49	.011115	.011631	.016267	79	.115754	.141633	.134915
50	.011744	.012096	.017116	80	.126474	.157750	.145768
51	.012429	.012622	.018005	81	.138164	.175615	.158716
52	.013187	.013217	.018786	82	.150873	.195366	.172301
53	.014047	.013890	.019911	83	.164676	.217135	.185770
54	.014979	.014650	.020941	84	.179638	.241048	.199030

TABLE XI.

EXPECTATION OF LIFE

According to various Tables of Mortality.

Age.	CANADA	UNITED STATES				GREAT BRITAIN			GERMANY	AUSTRALIA	
	Canada Life.	Mutual Life of New York.	Mutual Benefit of New Jersey.	American Experience.	Heavy American Officers.	Equitable.	Raw Life.	Twenty Years Purch... H	Gotha Life.	Australian Mutual Prov.	
										Assured Ages.	Low Ages.
20	46.249	44.99		42.20	43.069	41.670	42.90	42.061	42.22	47.121	45.823
21	45.462	44.26		41.53	42.359	40.974	42.16	41.326	41.46	46.284	44.973
22	44.673	43.53		40.85	41.646	40.266	41.42	40.603	40.77	45.440	44.121
23	43.881	42.80		40.17	40.930	39.555	40.67	39.879	40.06	44.595	43.265
24	43.089	42.07		39.49	40.211	38.840	39.91	39.147	39.42	43.748	42.410
25	42.294	41.33	40.906	38.81	39.492	38.123	39.17	38.405	38.64	42.899	41.558
26	41.498	40.59	40.162	38.12	38.766	37.411	38.45	37.658	37.83	42.050	40.708
27	40.701	39.84	39.415	37.43	38.040	36.696	37.72	36.908	37.04	41.203	39.865
28	39.902	39.09	38.663	36.73	37.312	35.977	36.99	36.162	36.20	40.360	39.027
29	39.103	38.34	37.913	36.03	36.582	35.255	36.26	35.419	35.47	39.518	38.192
30	38.303	37.59	37.158	35.33	35.850	34.530	35.52	34.681	34.69	38.682	37.365
31	37.502	36.83	36.402	34.63	35.117	33.809	34.78	33.946	33.91	37.851	36.543
32	36.700	36.07	35.643	33.92	34.383	33.084	34.04	33.213	33.14	37.028	35.728
33	35.898	35.31	34.883	33.21	33.646	32.364	33.29	32.481	32.36	36.208	34.918
34	35.096	34.55	34.121	32.50	32.910	31.647	32.54	31.748	31.59	35.397	34.117
35	34.298	33.78	33.358	31.78	32.172	30.934	31.79	31.016	30.80	34.590	33.317
36	33.494	33.01	32.593	31.07	31.434	30.217	31.05	30.286	29.92	33.785	32.521
37	32.693	32.24	31.828	30.35	30.696	29.503	30.31	29.560	29.22	32.980	31.728
38	31.891	31.47	31.061	29.62	29.957	28.793	29.58	28.838	28.46	32.179	30.938
39	31.096	30.70	30.295	28.90	29.219	28.092	28.85	28.118	27.71	31.379	30.448
40	30.299	29.93	29.530	28.18	28.482	27.395	28.13	27.399	26.94	30.585	29.364
41	29.505	29.15	28.764	27.45	27.747	26.694	27.40	26.679	26.17	29.798	28.583
42	28.713	28.38	27.999	26.72	27.013	25.994	26.66	25.956	25.41	29.019	27.813
43	27.924	27.61	27.234	26.00	26.280	25.290	25.93	25.233	24.66	28.247	27.048
44	27.137	26.83	26.472	25.27	25.550	24.581	25.19	24.511	23.89	27.481	26.290
45	26.355	26.06	25.711	24.54	24.822	23.873	24.46	23.792	23.13	26.721	25.538
46	25.576	25.29	24.952	23.81	24.090	23.174	23.75	23.079	22.40	25.961	24.790
47	24.801	24.52	24.196	23.08	23.377	22.469	23.04	22.375	21.66	25.210	24.042
48	24.032	23.76	23.444	22.36	22.660	21.766	22.34	21.679	20.95	24.461	23.299
49	23.268	22.99	22.693	21.63	21.948	21.065	21.66	20.989	20.22	23.716	22.561
50	22.509	22.23	21.949	20.91	21.241	20.362	20.98	20.306	19.51	22.975	21.820
51	21.757	21.48	21.209	20.20	20.539	19.662	20.30	19.627	18.80	22.236	21.100
52	21.012	20.73	20.474	19.49	19.843	18.977	19.61	18.951	18.10	21.502	20.378
53	20.275	19.98	19.745	18.79	19.154	18.302	18.97	18.284	17.43	20.769	19.655
54	19.545	19.24	19.022	18.09	18.471	17.643	18.31	17.618	16.71	20.035	18.930
55	18.824	18.51	18.306	17.40	17.707	16.989	17.66	16.962	16.08	19.305	18.201
56	18.112	17.78	17.597	16.72	17.130	16.310	17.01	16.316	15.41	18.577	17.480
57	17.409	17.06	16.898	16.05	16.473	15.705	16.36	15.679	14.77	17.855	16.765
58	16.717	16.35	16.207	15.39	15.825	15.091	15.72	15.052	14.15	17.140	16.054
59	16.035	15.65	15.523	14.74	15.187	14.491	15.08	14.435	13.53	16.434	15.363

TABLE XI.– Continued.

EXPECTATION OF LIFE

According to various Tables of Mortality.

Age.	CANADA.	UNITED STATES.				GREAT BRITAIN.			GERMANY	AUSTRALIA.	
	Canada Life.	Mutual Life of New York	Mutual Benefit of New Jersey.	American Experience.	Thirty American Offices.	Equitable.	Law Life.	Twenty British Offices. H^m	Gotha Life.	Australian Mutual Prov. d^th	
										Assumed Ages.	True Age.
60	15.365	14.96	14.854	14.10	14.559	13.911	14.44	13.830	12.95	15.736	14.692
61	14.707	14.28	14.193	13.47	13.942	13.347	13.81	13.237	12.36	15.046	14.026
62	14.061	13.62	13.545	12.86	13.336	12.789	13.19	12.659	11.79	14.365	13.374
63	13.429	12.96	12.908	12.26	12.743	12.231	12.58	12.095	11.23	13.696	12.754
64	12.810	12.32	12.284	11.67	12.162	11.680	12.00	11.547	10.67	13.049	12.170
65	12.203	11.70	11.673	11.10	11.595	11.131	11.43	11.012	10.15	12.429	11.608
66	11.615	11.08	11.076	10.54	11.040	10.609	10.89	10.489	9.64	11.841	11.086
67	11.039	10.49	10.494	10.00	10.500	10.106	10.36	9.977	9.17	11.280	10.589
68	10.480	9.91	9.927	9.47	9.974	9.618	9.86	9.475	8.72	10.754	10.107
69	9.936	9.35	9.376	8.97	9.463	9.146	9.37	8.980	8.25	10.233	9.628
70	9.408	8.80	8.841	8.48	8.967	8.699	8.90	8.495	7.83	9.716	9.177
71	8.897	8.27	8.322	8.00	8.486	8.259	8.44	8.026	7.40	9.201	8.729
72	8.403	7.76	7.820	7.55	8.021	7.827	7.98	7.575	6.99	8.692	8.307
73	7.926	7.27	7.335	7.11	7.572	7.406	7.53	7.148	6.60	8.151	7.869
74	7.467	6.80	6.868	6.68	7.138	6.999	7.10	6.749	6.21	7.620	7.417
75	7.025	6.35	6.418	6.27	6.721	6.609	6.68	6.376	5.88	7.100	6.924
76	6.600	5.92	5.986	5.88	6.320	6.236	6.28	6.017	5.55	6.569	6.413
77	6.193	5.51	5.572	5.49	5.934	5.860	5.91	5.674	5.21	6.041	5.872
78	5.804	5.11	5.177	5.11	5.565	5.487	5.56	5.344	4.88	5.571	5.384
79	5.431	4.74	4.799	4.74	5.211	5.120	5.23	5.025	4.59	5.135	4.951
80	5.077	4.39	4.439	4.39	4.873	4.754	4.92	4.719	4.20	4.733	4.589
81	4.710	4.06	4.097	4.05	4.550	4.406	4.62	4.433	3.99	4.401	4.294
82	4.419	3.74	3.773	3.71	4.242	4.086	4.34	4.171	3.69	4.134	4.080
83	4.116	3.45	3.463	3.39	3.947	3.791	4.07	3.930	3.31	3.890	3.882
84	3.828	3.17	3.172	3.08	3.666	3.574	3.84	3.713	3.23	3.671	3.693
85	3.557	2.91	2.898	2.77	3.396	3.387	3.64	3.511	2.99	3.479	3.505
86	3.302	2.67	2.640	2.47	3.137	3.207	3.46	3.310	2.72	3.282	3.304
87	3.661	2.43	2.398	2.18	2.885	3.027	3.28	3.101	2.63	3.066	3.075
88	2.836	2.22	2.171	1.91	2.637	2.890	3.13	2.884	2.66	2.841	2.835
89	2.625	2.05	1.958	1.66	2.386	2.803	2.98	2.634	2.32	2.607	2.612
90	2.127	1.87	1.760	1.42	2.166	2.559	2.84	2.357	2.26	2.359	2.365
91	2.243	1.71	1.576	1.19	1.980	2.316	2.63	2.077	1.93	2.093	2.101
92	2.072	1.56	1.404	.93	1.808	2.042	2.43	1.795	2.24	1.817	1.826
93	1.910	1.43	1.231	.80	1.643	1.750	2.19	1.496	1.75	1.535	1.547
94	1.763	1.30	1.096	.61	1.488	1.375	1.88	1.204	.73	1.245	1.258
95	1.625	1.19	.959	.50	1.338	1.055	1.49	.930	.50	.943	.962
96	1.491	1.08	.833		1.176	.750	1.02	.684		.633	.652
97	1.362	.98	.716		1.033	.500	.50	.500		.500	.500

TABLE XII.

Canada Life Annual Rates of Mortality compared with those of other Tables.

GRADUATED TABLES USED.

Age	Canada Life	American Experience	Three Americas Offices	Institute of Actuaries Hm	Mutual Life of New York	Mutual Benefit of New Jersey	Rate of Canada Life Mortality vs.				
							Mutual of Benefit	Inst. of Actuaries Offices	American Experience Hm	Mutual Life of New York	Mutual Benefit of New Jersey
20	.00463	.00781	.00676	.00635	.00611		.50	.69	.73	.73	
21	.00467	.00786	.00681	.00673	.00637		.59	.66	.69	.71	
22	.00471	.00701	.00686	.00683	.00639		.60	.69	.69	.70	
23	.00475	.00796	.00691	.00676	.00631		.60	.69	.70	.76	
24	.00480	.00801	.00697	.00664	.00633		.60	.69	.72	.77	
25	.00486	.00807	.00703	.00663	.00628	.00620	.60	.60	.73	.77	.77
26	.00492	.00813	.00712	.00660	.00633	.00634	.61	.60	.74	.78	.78
27	.00499	.00820	.00716	.00690	.00636	.00610	.61	.69	.72	.78	.78
28	.00506	.00826	.00728	.00717	.00640	.00646	.61	.70	.71	.79	.78
29	.00511	.00835	.00739	.00743	.00646	.00653	.62	.70	.69	.80	.79
30	.00524	.00843	.00740	.00772	.00651	.00660	.62	.70	.68	.80	.79
31	.00534	.00851	.00762	.00702	.00658	.00660	.63	.70	.67	.81	.80
32	.00545	.00861	.00773	.00811	.01065	.00675	.63	.70	.67	.82	.80
33	.00557	.00872	.00782	.00820	.00673	.00686	.64	.71	.67	.82	.81
34	.00570	.00883	.00803	.00830	.00682	.00700	.65	.71	.67	.84	.81
35	.00585	.00895	.00834	.00877	.00691	.00713	.65	.71	.67	.85	.82
36	.00601	.00905	.00837	.00811	.00703	.00727	.66	.72	.66	.87	.82
37	.00619	.00923	.00836	.00846	.00716	.00744	.67	.72	.65	.86	.83
38	.00639	.00941	.00885	.00878	.00730	.00762	.68	.72	.65	.85	.83
39	.00661	.00959	.00908	.01008	.00740	.00779	.69	.73	.66	.84	.83
40	.00685	.00976	.00936	.01031	.00761	.00803	.70	.73	.66	.90	.86
41	.00712	.01001	.00965	.01049	.00781	.00824	.71	.72	.68	.91	.89
42	.00731	.01023	.01006	.01073	.00806	.00851	.72	.74	.66	.91	.85
43	.00754	.01052	.01033	.01115	.00831	.00880	.74	.75	.70	.93	.85
44	.00809	.01083	.01170	.01156	.00889	.00912	.75	.75	.70	.91	.89
45	.00838	.01116	.01170	.01219	.00890	.00948	.76	.75	.72	.93	.89
46	.00892	.01156	.01160	.01292	.00925	.00988	.77	.76	.64	.90	.90
47	.00940	.01200	.01223	.01330	.00964	.01052	.78	.77	.67	.95	.91
48	.00992	.01261	.01261	.01441	.01006	.01081	.70	.77	.67	.98	.92
49	.01050	.01311	.01349	.01372	.01057	.01130	.80	.78	.66	.99	.93
50	.01113	.01378	.01416	.01393	.01111	.01190	.81	.77	.70	1.00	.93
51	.01183	.01454	.01466	.01605	.01172	.01263	.82	.76	.71	1.03	.94
52	.01261	.01391	.01681	.01735	.01241	.01335	.83	.76	.72	1.02	.94

TABLE XII.—Continued.

Canada Life Annual Rates of Mortality compared with those of other Tables.

GRADUATED TABLES USED.

Age.	Canada Life.	American Experience.	Thirty American Offices.	Institute of Actuaries Hm.	Mutual Life of New York.	Mutual Benefit of New Jersey.	Ratio of Canada Life Mortality to				
							American Experience.	Thirty American Offices.	Institute of Actuaries Hm.	Mutual Life of New York.	Mutual Benefit of New Jersey.
53	.01348	.01633	.01675	01860	.01317	.01420	.83	.80	.72	1.02	.95
54	.01443	.01740	.01778	01973	.01403	.01511	.83	.81	.73	1.03	.95
55	.01547	.01857	.01893	.02103	.01498	.01613	.83	.82	.74	1.03	.96
56	.01661	.01989	.02017	.02245	.01605	.01725	.84	.82	.74	1.03	.96
57	.01787	.02134	.02156	.02399	.01725	.01850	.84	.83	.74	1.04	.97
58	.01926	.02294	.02306	.02563	.01858	.01988	.84	.84	.75	1.04	.97
59	.02079	.02472	.02471	.02754	.02008	.02141	.84	.84	.75	1.04	.97
60	.02248	.02669	.02653	.02968	.02175	.02311	.84	.85	.76	1.03	.97
61	.02434	.02888	.02853	.03204	.02361	.02500	.84	.85	.76	1.03	.97
62	.02638	.03129	.03070	.03464	.02569	.02709	.84	.86	.76	1.03	.97
63	.02863	.03394	.03311	.03749	.02802	.02942	.84	.86	.76	1.02	.97
64	.03110	.03687	.03574	.04031	.03062	.03199	.84	.87	.77	1.02	.97
65	.03382	.04013	.03864	.04343	.03351	.03485	.84	.88	.78	1.01	.97
66	.03681	.04371	.04179	.04657	.03675	.03801	.84	.88	.79	1.00	.97
67	.04010	.04765	.04528	.04989	.04035	.04153	.84	.89	.80	.99	.97
68	.04371	.05200	.04901	.05323	.04437	.04543	.84	.89	.82	.99	.96
69	.04768	.05676	.05324	.05734	.04885	.04975	.84	.90	.83	.98	.96
70	.05204	.06199	.05778	.06219	.05384	.05454	.84	.90	.84	.97	.95
71	.05683	.06767	.06278	.06805	.05939	.05986	.84	.90	.84	.96	.95
72	.06207	.07323	.06822	.07494	.06557	.06576	.84	.91	.83	.95	.94
73	.06783	.08018	.07415	.08286	.07243	.07230	.85	.91	.82	.94	.94
74	.07413	.08703	.08071	.09120	.08006	.07956	.85	.92	.81	.93	.93
75	.08104	.09437	.08779	.09836	.08852	08761	.86	.92	.82	.92	.93
76	.08860	.10231	.09550	.10637	.09789	.09654	.87	.93	.83	.91	.92
77	.09686	.11106	.10300	.11469	.10827	.10644	.87	.93	.84	.89	.91
78	.10589	.12083	.11318	.12321	.11975	.11743	.88	.94	.86	.88	.90
79	.11573	.13173	.12319	.13306	.13242	.12961	.88	.94	.87	.87	.89
80	.12647	.14447	.13407	.14165	.14638	.14313	.88	.94	.87	.86	.88
81	.13816	.15861	.14583	.15804	.16174	.15812	.87	.95	.87	.85	.87
82	.15087	.17430	.15870	.17135	.17861	.17414	.87	.95	.88	.84	.87
83	.16168	.19156	.17246	.18585	.19709	.19318	.86	.95	.89	.84	.85
84	.17964	.21136	.18752	.19888	.21727	.21364	.85	.96	.90	.83	.84
85	.19583	.23555	.20363	.20989	.23927	.23032	.83	.96	.93	.82	.83

TABLE XIII.

Exposed to Risk and Died in quinquennial groups of ages,
Also the Expected Deaths by other Tables of Mortality.

| Completed Ages | Canada Life. | | United States | | | | | Great Britain. | | Germany | Australia. | |
	Exposed to Risk	Died	Mutual Life of New York.	Mutual Benefit of New Jersey.	Connecticut Mutual (Males.)	American Experience	Thirty American Offices (Male.)	Hm. Table.	Scottish Widows' Fund.	Gotha Life.	Australian Mutual Prov. Society. At Assumed Ages.	At Actual Ages.
20-24	16931.	81	109.	118.7	134.6	133.9	116.3	116.5	72.8	118.3	57.6	56.9
25-29	38443.3	194	234.9	266.	280.3	315.2	262.2	265.3	176.8	227.2	151.1	161.1
30-34	50229.7	274	333.5	341.	344.1	433.	350.1	412.4	266.2	342.1	243.1	267.2
35-39	51450.3	353	394.1	369.9	392.6	475.9	406.5	490.3	360.2	410.1	317.4	344.7
40-44	45226.	321	349.6	389.8	396.2	464.5	404.7	482.6	402.5	430.1	358.6	380.4
45-49	35310.	331	351.3	352.4	363.	425.8	380.6	480.9	360.2	456.2	352.	377.8
50-54	25124.7	315	312.	339.2	332.7	388.4	347.7	436.2	354.3	438.2	313.8	353.3
55-59	16229.7	288	267.8	304.6	289.4	347.8	302.7	389.4	360.3	412.9	257.4	282.9
60-64	9083.7	245	233.6	245.3	240.4	285.	243.4	315.8	289.8	338.6	208.5	248.3
65-69	4646.7	176	189.	185.8	179.8	221.5	177.3	233.1	203.5	267.6	191.6	224.5
70-74	2079.7	124	124.2	135.8	107.6	152.3	115.5	152.4	142.5	175.4	105.3	137.6
75-79	753.	76	74.6	75.8	75.5	82.8	63.5	82.8	72.9	91.5	65.2	56.2
20-79	295507.8	2748.	2973.6	3124.3	3136.2	3726.1	3190.5	3857.7	3062.	3708.2	2621.6	2890.9
Percentage of Canada Life to other Tables			92.4	88.	87.6	73.8	86.1	71.2	89.7	74.1	104.8	95.1

TABLE XIV.

Annual Rate of Mortality per cent. in quinquennial groups of ages.

Group of Ages.	CANADA		UNITED STATES.				GREAT BRITAIN.		GERMANY.	AUSTRALIA.	
	Canada Life.	Mutual Life of New York	Mutual Benefit of New Jersey	Connecticut Mutual. (Male.)	American Experience.	Thirty American Tables. (Male.)	Institute of Actuaries H^m	Scottish Widows' Fund.	Gotha Life.	Australian Mutual Prov. Society. At Assumed Ages.	At Actual Ages.
20-24	.480	.544	.501	.795	.791	.687	.688	.430	.699	.340	.336
25-29	.505	.611	.692	.729	.820	.682	.690	.460	.591	.393	.419
30-34	.545	.664	.679	.685	.862	.697	.821	.530	.681	.484	.532
35-39	.628	.766	.710	.763	.925	.790	.953	.700	.797	.617	.670
40-44	.711	.773	.862	.876	1.027	.939	1.067	.890	.951	.793	.841
45-49	.936	.995	.908	1.028	1.206	1.078	1.362	1.020	1.292	.997	1.070
50-54	1.254	1.242	1.350	1.324	1.546	1.384	1.436	1.410	1.744	1.249	1.406
55-59	1.575	1.850	1.877	1.783	2.143	1.865	2.399	2.220	2.544	1.586	1.743
60-64	2.701	2.572	2.700	2.647	3.138	2.680	3.477	3.190	3.728	2.295	2.733
65-69	3.780	4.067	3.919	3.870	3.764	3.816	5.017	4.380	5.260	4.124	4.831
70-74	5.979	5.974	6.532	5.174	7.321	5.556	7.329	6.850	8.432	5.062	6.647
75-79	10.992	9.993	10.060	10.033	10.998	8.437	10.990	9.680	12.450	8.659	7.468

TABLE XV.

Actual Deaths by years of Assurance in the Canada Life Assurance Company,

Compared with Expected Deaths by other Tables

ALL AGES COMBINED.

Year Assurance	Expected Risk of Death	H.G.	Mutual Life of New York	Combined Mutual (Males)	Hunt Experience	Gov. Table	Heavy Assurance Tables (Males)	Northamp. Very Healthy Lives (1873)
1	34036	142	169.5	253.	205.5	156.5	254.	471.5
2	27534	158	178.5	224.5	200.	210.	233.	432.5
3	24475	148	189.5	193.	210.	243	225.5	155.
4	22060	140	188.5	204.5	213.5	254	230.5	429.5
5	19751	125	183.5	189.	209.	260	215.5	435.
6	17595	139	180.5	199.5	197	231	203.5	131.
7	16381	134	160.5	178.	167.5	235.5	193.5	132.
8	14861	135	161.5	162.5	168.	221.5	182.	126.5
9	13505	123	135.5	165.	161.	207.	161.5	134.5
10	17306	112	141.5	148.5	140.5	200.5	151.5	122.
11	11081	105	135.	146.	152.	199.5	141.	103.5
12	10043	104	142.5	132.5	132	179.5	138.	165.5
13	8908	80	121.	121.5	124	177.5	133.	168
14	7870	85	82.5	121.	122	165.	110.5	93.5
15	7038	89	86.	115.	106.5	160.5	103.	91.
16	6323	89	91.5	105.5	92.5	154	93.5	85.
17	5733	74	97.	123.5	103	146	91.	85.5
18	5155	70	96.	80.	85.5	123.5	55.5	58.
19	4588	64	58.5	91.5	72.5	130.5	76.5	60.
20	4073	59	77.5	73.	86.5	116.	78.5	58.
21	3542	65	57.5	77.5	75.5	105	68.5	57.5
22	2936	55	62.	71.5	71.	95.	64	70.
23	2413	47	64.	55.	66.	83	59.5	54.
24	1911	33	57.	58.5	62.	64.5	51.	42.
25	1637	26	53.5	46.	45.5	61	35.	47.5
26	1438	34	38.	43.	39.	50.	10.	12.
27	1266	44	38.	36.	38.	50.	19.	33.
28	1009	29	24.5	70.	30.	44.	11.5	71.
29	980	48	26.	34.	42.	44.5	17.	21.5
30	858	53	24.5	35.	34.5	41.	23.	32.5
1-30	291738	2572	3235.5	3320.5	3481.	4143	3502.5	2611.5
1-5	127875	685	906.0	1071.	1041.	1122.5	1198.5	6353.
6-30	163863	1901	2291.	2255.5	2437.	3310.5	2414	1958.

TABLE XVI.

Annual Rate of Mortality by Years of Assurance.

ALL AGES COMBINED.

Year of Assurance.	Exposed to Risk of Death.	Died.	Mortality per cent per annum. Canada Life.	Mortality per cent per annum.					
				Mutual Life of New York.	Connecticut Mutual. (Males.)	Mutual Benefit.	Hm Table.	Thirty American Offices. (Males.)	Australian Mutual Prov. Society. (1881.)
1	34046	112	.329	.498	.746	.604	.459	.629	.363
2	27534	158	.574	.649	.816	.749	.762	.810	.482
3	24478	148	.605	.761	.812	.858	.989	.921	.543
4	22066	140	.631	.855	.927	.968	1.150	1.000	.586
5	19751	125	.633	.928	.936	1.058	1.316	1.091	.684
6	17898	139	.777	1.008	1.114	1.101	1.308	1.136	.732
7	16384	134	.818	1.035	1.086	1.021	1.425	1.168	.812
8	14861	135	.908	1.107	1.127	1.131	1.489	1.225	.852
9	13508	123	.911	1.002	1.242	1.192	1.534	1.196	.995
10	12306	112	.910	1.151	1.207	1.141	1.630	1.231	.991
11	11081	105	.948	1.220	1.262	1.370	1.801	1.273	.934
12	10043	104	1.036	1.419	1.320	1.312	1.789	1.336	1.049
13	8908	80	.898	1.360	1.365	1.392	1.992	1.491	1.214
14	7870	83	1.055	1.050	1.536	1.553	2.132	1.406	1.188
15	7036	89	1.265	1.223	1.635	1.514	2.282	1.464	1.290
16	6323	89	1.408	1.444	1.719	1.461	2.439	1.477	1.376
17	5733	74	1.291	1.691	2.155	1.794	2.551	1.727	1.489
18	5155	70	1.358	1.861	1.550	1.662	2.398	1.716	1.707
19	4588	64	1.395	1.861	1.989	1.577	2.845	1.664	1.442
20	4073	59	1.449	1.900	1.791	2.128	2.842	1.923	1.921
21	3547	65	1.833	1.618	2.180	2.131	2.964	1.934	1.898
22	2956	55	1.861	2.125	2.124	2.402	3.317	2.162	2.375
23	2413	47	1.948	2.644	2.288	2.864	3.432	2.460	2.237
24	1911	37	1.936	2.992	3.060	3.235	3.376	2.670	2.210
25	1637	46	2.810	3.278	2.816	2.779	3.712	2.751	2.908
26	1438	35	2.433	2.634	3.139	4.091	3.902	2.799	3.069
27	1266	44	3.476	3.016	2.834	2.992	4.650	3.078	2.756
28	1090	29	2.661	2.252	2.681	2.773	4.045	2.892	1.942
29	980	13	1.388	2.632	3.453	4.288	3.526	3.543	2.194
30	858	33	3.846	2.195	1.664	3.995	5.153	2.692	3.790
1-30	291738	2577	.883	1.081	1.209	1.193	1.519	1.197	.905
1-5	127875	683	.534	.709	.838	.816	.878	.859	.511
6-30	163863	1894	1.156	1.372	1.499	1.487	2.019	1.461	1.213

TABLE XVII.

Ratio of Actual Deaths to Expected Deaths by other Mortality Tables.

ALL AGES COMBINED

Age at Anniversary	Actuaries (Combined) of New York	Carlisle Mortal. (Males)	Mutual Trusts of New Jersey	Elta Table	Thirty American Offices (Males)	American Mutual (Males)
1	60.1	45.1	54.5	21.6	52.3	95.7
2	88.3	70.4	76.2	75.2	70.9	119.2
3	79.4	74.4	70.5	61.2	65.6	111.3
4	74.3	68.5	65.6	55.1	63.5	108.1
5	68.1	66.1	59.8	48.1	58	92.6
6	77	69.7	70.6	59.4	68.5	106.1
7	79.1	75.3	80.	57.4	70.	106.8
8	82.1	80.6	80.4	60.9	74.2	106.7
9	90.8	73.2	76.4	59.3	76.2	91.4
10	79.7	75.4	79.7	55.9	73.9	91.8
11	77.8	75.	69.1	52.6	74.5	101.4
12	73.	78.5	78.8	57.9	77.6	98.6
13	66.1	65.8	64.5	45.1	60.2	74.1
14	100.6	68.6	68.	49.4	75.1	88.8
15	105.5	77.4	83.6	55.5	86.4	97.8
16	97.3	82.	96.2	57.8	95.8	102.3
17	76.3	59.9	74.8	50.7	74.7	86.5
18	72.9	87.5	84.6	56.7	79.1	79.5
19	74.9	69.9	88.3	49.	85.7	97.
20	76.1	80.8	68.2	50.9	75.2	75.6
21	113.	83.9	86.1	61.9	94.9	96.3
22	87.3	76.9	77.5	56.1	85.9	78.6
23	73.4	85.5	68.1	56.6	79.	87.
24	64.0	63.2	59.7	57.4	72.5	88.1
25	86.	100.	104.1	75.1	102.2	90.8
26	91.1	77.8	50.3	62.5	87.5	79.5
27	115.8	122.7	115.8	74.9	112.8	125.7
28	118.1	100.	96.7	63.9	97.1	138.1
29	165.4	126.5	102.4	96.6	122.9	100.
30	153.5	94.3	96.7	75.	143.5	101.5
1-30	81.7	73.1	74.	58.1	75.6	97.0
1-5	75.3	63.8	60.1	62.8	62.2	103.5
6-30	84.2	72.1	77.7	57.2	78.8	95.3

TABLE XVIII.

PART 1.—Experience during the First Five Years of Assurance.

Actual Ages	Canada Life		Expected Deaths by					
	Exposed	Died	Mutual Benefit of New Jersey	Connecticut Mutual (Males)	Mutual Life of New York	Scottish Widows Fund	H M (m 5) Table	Australian Mutual Prov. Society, 1888 (Assumed Ages)
19-24	17086.	83.5	119	141.5	112.	68.5	111.	54.5
25-29	30109.5	138.5	211.5	205.5	170.5	114.5	185.	116.
30-34	28300.	123.5	175.	181.	168.5	127.5	210.5	123.5
35-39	21731.	112.5	152.	153.5	151.5	119.5	175.5	124.5
40-44	14467.	73.	120.	119.	93.	94.	128.5	96.5
45-49	8492.5	65.	81.	76.5	78.	65.5	100.	64.5
50-54	4537.5	42.5	59.	52.5	46.5	36.	56.5	50.
55-59	1958.	23.5	34.	36.5	28.5	36.	38.	20.
60-64	657.5	13.5	14.	15.5	15.	15.	19.	17.5
65-69	209.5	4.5	7.	5.	9.	7.5	8.	5.5
19-69	127548.5	680.	972.5	986.5	877.5	684.	1032.	672.5

PART 2.—Experience excluding the First Five Years of Assurance.

Actual Ages	Canada Life		Expected Deaths by					
	Exposed	Died	Mutual Benefit of New Jersey	Connecticut Mutual (Males)	Mutual Life of New York	Scottish Widows Fund	H M (5) Table	Australian Mutual Prov. Society, 1888 (Assumed Ages)
24-29	8510.	55.5	54.	80.5	75.	67.	79.5	35.
30-34	21929.5	150.5	169.5	172.	187.5	142.5	207.	121.5
35-39	29719.5	210.5	219.	248.	261.	238.	319.5	196.
40-44	30759.	248.5	271.5	282.5	270.5	304.5	358.	269.5
45-49	26817.5	265.5	273.	296.	282.5	289.5	384.	296.5
50-54	20587.	272.5	281.5	287.	283.5	313.	386.5	267.
55-59	14271.5	264.5	272.5	251.	249.	322.5	356.5	243.
60-64	8426.5	231.5	236.5	227.5	225.	274.5	301.	190.
65-69	4437.	171.5	181.	176.5	179.5	195.5	228.5	185.
70-74	2061.5	121.5	135.	166.5	126.	142.5	153.	105.
75-79	753.	76.	76.	75.	75.5	73.	84.	65.5
80-84	166.5	28.5	25.5	23.	21.5	24.	27.5	18.5
85-88	30.5	5.	8.5	5.	2.5	7.	7.	6.5
24-88	168469.	2101.5	2203.5	2230.5	2239.	2393.5	2892.	1999.

TABLE XIX.

PART 1 —Annual Rate of Mortality per cent
First Five Years of Assurance.

Ages	Canada Life	Mutual Benefit of New Jersey	Connecticut Mutual (Males)	Mutual Life of New York	Scottish Widows Fund	HM Table	Assured Premium Society (At same Ages)
19-24	.429	.692	.829	.955	.47	.643	.319
25-29	.460	.797	.633	.862	.38	.613	.385
30-34	.450	.609	.642	.593	.45	.543	.330
35-39	.548	.700	.720	.607	.55	.828	.371
40-44	.593	.820	.823	.670	.65	.880	.603
45-49	.793	.953	.699	.921	.77	1.127	.736
50-54	.917	1.295	1.157	1.028	.76	1.247	1.104
55-59	1.200	1.239	1.375	1.450	1.53	1.042	1.652
60-64	2.053	2.154	7.393	2.270	2.35	2.905	2.678
65-69	2.148	3.255	2.325	4.169	3.62	5.532	2.589
70-74	..	..	3.557	4.515	1.03	3.603	..
75-77	..	..	16.603	7.613	10.43	6.530	..
19-77	.533	.850	.838	.743	.605	.957	.533

PART 2.—Annual Rate of Mortality per cent.
Excluding First Five Years of Assurance.

Ages	Canada Life	Mutual Benefit of New Jersey	Connecticut Mutual (Males.)	Mutual Life of New York.	Scottish Widows Fund.	HM Table.	Assured Premium Society (At same Ages)
24-29	.651	.637	.947	.881	.79	.937	.414
30-34	.687	.774	.784	.854	.65	.943	.555
35-39	.709	.737	.834	.879	.80	1.075	.600
40-44	.807	.882	.919	.879	.99	1.164	.876
45-49	.990	1.018	1.103	1.053	1.08	1.432	1.105
50-54	1.324	1.367	1.395	1.377	1.52	1.878	1.296
55-59	1.855	1.910	1.757	1.743	2.26	2.497	1.702
60-64	2.750	2.809	2.698	2.669	3.26	3.571	2.253
65-69	3.861	4.082	3.982	4.015	4.41	5.130	4.172
70-74	5.904	6.542	5.171	6.106	6.91	7.411	5.103
75-79	10.106	10.060	10.000	10.050	9.68	11.127	8.718
80-84	17.258	15.318	13.669	12.521	14.38	16.620	11.455
85-88	16.013	27.248	16.364	7.602	22.33	22.870	21.622
24-88	1.248	1.415	1.380	1.251	1.97	2.193	1.006

TABLE XX.

PART 1.—Annual Rates of Mortality per cent. for Central Ages at entry, by quinquennial years of assurance.

Central Age at entry.	Years of Assurance.						
	1-5	6-10	11-15	16-20	21-25	26-30	Over 30.
20	.566	.644	.720				
25	.450	.639	.637	.898	1.345	1.362	
30	.435	.673	.784	.956	1.465	2.591	3.629
35	.499	.840	1.085	1.146	1.933	4.007	4.646
40	.508	.870	1.157	1.732	2.888	4.018	6.277
45	.732	1.335	1.384	2.304	3.279	5.381	13.111
50	.913	1.994	2.692	3.380	7.407	11.297	20.536
55	1.089	2.527	3.086	6.977	9.453		
60	2.038	2.387	6.011				

PART 2.—Annual Rates of Mortality per cent. for Ages at Exposure, by quinquennial years of assurance.

Age at Exposure (m-d)	Years of Assurance.						
	1-5	6-10	11-15	16-20	21-25	26-30	Over 30.
20-24	.475						
25-29	.475	.638					
30-34	.436	.655	.731				
35-39	.513	.662	.630	1.163			
40-44	.503	.809	.837	.825	.571		
45-49	.717	.920	.851	1.083	1.320	2.083	
50-54	.965	1.339	1.277	1.035	1.489	1.623	1.277
55-59	1.157	1.811	1.481	1.624	2.000	2.222	2.260
60-64	1.972	2.335	2.488	2.451	2.516	3.913	3.028
65-69	2.183	3.110	3.758	3.279	4.290	4.417	3.552
70-74		5.618	5.769	6.920	5.045	4.910	5.760
75-79			10.959	12.632	11.278	7.966	

TABLE XXI.

Commutation and Life Annuity Values, Canada Life Experience,

Excluding the First Five Years of Assurance.

INTEREST AT 4%.

Age.	D_x	N_x	a_x	Age.	D_x	N_x	a_x
25	38005.	708880.	18.6523	65	4839.1	41545.5	8.5854
26	36309.	672571.	18.5235	66	4493.5	37052.0	8.2458
27	34689	637882.	18.3886	67	4150.7	32892.3	7.9074
28	33140.	604742.	18.2481	68	3837.7	29054.6	7.5708
29	31650.	573092.	18.1072	69	3527.6	25527.0	7.2364
30	30243.	542849.	17.9496	70	3229.3	22297.7	6.9048
31	28889.	513960.	17.7909	71	2942.9	19454.8	6.5768
32	27594.	486366.	17.6258	72	2668.6	16686.2	6.2528
33	26355.	460011.	17.4544	73	2406.5	14279.7	5.9338
34	25171.	434840.	17.2754	74	2157.0	12122.7	5.6202
35	24038.	410802.	17.0897	75	1920.3	10202.4	5.3129
36	22954.	387848.	16.8968	76	1696.8	8505.6	5.0127
37	21916.	365932.	16.6970	77	1487.0	7018.6	4.7200
38	20922.	345010.	16.4903	78	1291.3	5727.3	4.4353
39	19971.	325039.	16.2755	79	1110.1	4617.23	4.1593
40	19059.	305980.	16.0544	80	943.91	3673.32	3.8916
41	18185.	287795.	15.8260	81	792.82	2880.50	3.6332
42	17346.	270449.	15.5914	82	657.00	2223.50	3.3843
43	16542.	253907.	15.3192	83	536.42	1687.08	3.1451
44	15771.	238136.	15.0996	84	430.85	1256.23	2.9157
45	15031.	223105.	14.8430	85	339.86	916.37	2.6963
46	14320.	208785.	14.5800	86	262.79	653.58	2.4871
47	13732.	195053.	14.3043	87	198.78	454.80	2.2880
48	12981.	182072.	14.0260	88	146.76	308.04	2.0989
49	12349.	169723.	13.7439	89	105.50	202.546	1.9199
50	11742.	157981.	13.4544	90	73.629	128.917	1.7509
51	11158.	146823.	13.1585	91	49.743	79.174	1.5917
52	10596.	136227.	12.8565	92	32.421	46.753	1.4421
53	10054.	126172.8	12.5495	93	20.312	26.441	1.3017
54	9531.4	116641.4	12.2376	94	12.182	14.2593	1.1705
55	9027.5	107613.9	11.9207	95	6.9626	7.2967	1.0480
56	8541.3	99072.6	11.5992	96	3.7738	3.5229	.9335
57	8071.8	91000.8	11.2739	97	1.9291	1.59382	.8262
58	7618.4	83382.4	10.9449	98	.92448	.66931	.7240
59	7180.0	76202.4	10.6131	99	.41258	.25676	.6223
60	6756.3	69446.1	10.2787	100	.17022	.086545	.5084
61	6346.7	63099.4	9.9121	101	.064400	.022145	.3439
62	5950.4	57149.0	9.6512	102	.022145		
63	5567.4	51581.6	9.2649				
64	5197.0	46384.6	8.9253				

TABLE XXIV.

Rate of Discontinuance per cent. by years of Assurance.

Years of Assurance	Mutual Life of New York	Australian Mutual Provident Society. (Males)	Thirty American Offices. (Male Lives.)	H^m Table.	Twenty-three German Offices.
0	5.4	12.5	9.58	2.7	...
1	12.0	13.6	18.26	7.0	10.2
2	6.8	4.1	10.38	4.9	5.3
3	4.8	2.4	8.40	4.1	4.1
4	3.8	2.4	6.97	3.3	3.1
5	3.3	2.5	6.08	2.8	2.7
6	2.6	2.3	5.02	2.4	2.1
7	3.8	2.2	5.40	3.6	1.8
8	2.0	2.0	3.45	1.8	1.5
9	2.2	1.8	2.93	1.5	1.3
10	1.8	1.8	2.76	1.5	1.3
11	2.0	1.7	2.41	1.5	1.2
12	1.9	1.7	1.91	1.4	1.0
13	1.9	1.4	1.59	1.2	.9
14	2.1	1.6	1.79	1.2	.8
15	1.4	1.8	1.13	1.1	.9
16	1.6	1.6	1.13	1.0	.6
17	1.4	1.5	.89	.9	.7
18	1.3	1.7	.88	.8	.5
19	1.0	1.5	.79	.8	.5
20	1.2	1.8	.79	.8	.7
21	1.3	1.8	.77	.7	.5
22	1.4	1.6	.70	.8	.4
23	1.4	1.2	.63	.6	.6
24	.6	1.6	.45	.6	.7
25	.5	1.6	.44	.7	.4
26	.9	1.8	.83	.6	.5
27	.9	1.5	.54	.4	.7
28	.4	1.3	.70	.5	.6
29	2.4	1.3	1.36	.4	.5
30	.9	1.4	.60	.3	.4
31		.8		.4	.5
32		1.1		.5	.7
33		2.7		.5	1.0
34		.0		.2	.6
35		.0		.6	.5
36		0.2		.4	.4
37		3.1		.0	.9
38		0		.3	1.0
39		.0		.0	1.5
40				.4	1.3
41				.5	.0
42				.0	.0
43				1.3	2.8
44				.0	3.7

TABLE XXV.

Discontinuances in Quinquennial Periods.

Age at Entry	First Five Years			Second Five Years			Third Five Years			Fourth Five Years			Fifth Five Years			Sixth Five Years			Over Thirty Years		
	Exposed to Risk of Discontinuance	Discontinuances	Discontinuances per cent.	Exposed to Risk of Discontinuance	Discontinuances	Discontinuances per cent.	Exposed to Risk of Discontinuance	Discontinuances	Discontinuances per cent.	Exposed to Risk of Discontinuance	Discontinuances	Discontinuances per cent.	Exposed to Risk of Discontinuance	Discontinuances	Discontinuances per cent.	Exposed to Risk of Discontinuance	Discontinuances	Discontinuances per cent.	Exposed to Risk of Discontinuance	Discontinuances	Discontinuances per cent.
20-24	27362	2191	8.01	12309	275	2.22	6821	83	1.22	3694	23	.64	1535	7	.46	611	1	.16	566	3	.53
25-29	35101	2705	7.71	18004	354	1.96	10747	131	1.22	6164	48	.78	2949	26	.88	1312	11	.82	1131	5	.44
30-34	30372	2251	7.41	16004	382	2.39	9968	113	1.14	6011	50	.83	3076	23	.75	1483	6	.40	1251	6	.48
35-39	22256	1537	6.91	12109	252	2.08	7696	104	1.35	4554	36	.79	2222	18	.81	963	3	.31	834	5	.59
40-44	13031	890	6.34	7600	174	2.29	4707	43	.91	2774	24	.87	1327	5	.38	629	1	.16	466	1	.21
45-49	8078	436	5.40	4407	96	2.18	2588	31	1.20	1392	12	.86	632	2	.32	251	4	1.59	131	2	1.53
50-54	3930	219	5.57	2101	32	1.52	1199	13	1.09	560	8	1.43	223	0	.15	64	1	1.52	21	0	.00
55-59	1675	79	4.72	833	15	1.80	406	5	1.23	166	2	1.20	40	0	.00	3	0	.00	6	0	.00
60 & ov'r	635	31	4.88	259	6	2.32	99	2	2.02	29	0	.00	8	0	.00	5	0	.00	0	0	.00
All ages	143442	10339	7.21	73816	1586	2.15	44162	525	1.19	25254	203	.80	12010	82	.68	5353	27	.50	4376	22	.50

TABLE XXVI.

Comparison of the Rates of Discontinuance per cent. in groups of Years of Assurance and groups of Ages at Entry.

Australian Mutual Provident Society (1888), and Mutual Life of New York (1873).

Ages at Entry.	First Five Years.		Second Five Years.		Third Five Years.		Fourth Five Years.		Fifth Five Years.		Sixth Five Years.	
	A. M. P. Society.	Mutual Life of New York.	A. M. P. Society.	Mutual Life of New York.	A. M. P. Society.	Mutual Life of New York.	A. M. P. Society.	Mutual Life of New York.	A. M. P. Society.	Mutual Life of New York.	A. M. P. Society.	Mutual Life of New York.
20-24	9.1	10.3	2.1	3.8	1.5	1.8	.9	1.5	.9	.9	.7	.6
25-29	8.7	7.8	2.0	3.2	1.5	1.7	1.0	1.1	1.2	1.1	2.1	.5
30-34	7.3	6.2	2.1	3.0	1.5	1.3	1.5	1.4	1.6	1.2	1.3	.3
35-39	6.5	5.8	2.0	2.8	1.6	2.1	1.8	1.4	1.9	1.3	1.7	.6
40-44	5.7	5.3	2.2	2.8	1.7	2.1	1.9	1.4	2.1	1.4	1.3	.6
45-49	5.5	5.0	2.4	2.5	1.9	2.1	2.3	1.0	2.0	1.1	1.1	1.2
50-54	4.5	4.7	2.2	2.3	2.3	1.8	2.4	1.6	1.2	1.4	1.6	5.1
55-59	4.8	4.7	2.4	1.4	2.3	1.6	1.9	.9	2.3	2.5	2.6	
60 & over.	5.6	3.3	4.5	3.3	3.1	3.2	5.5		6.1	..	28.6	

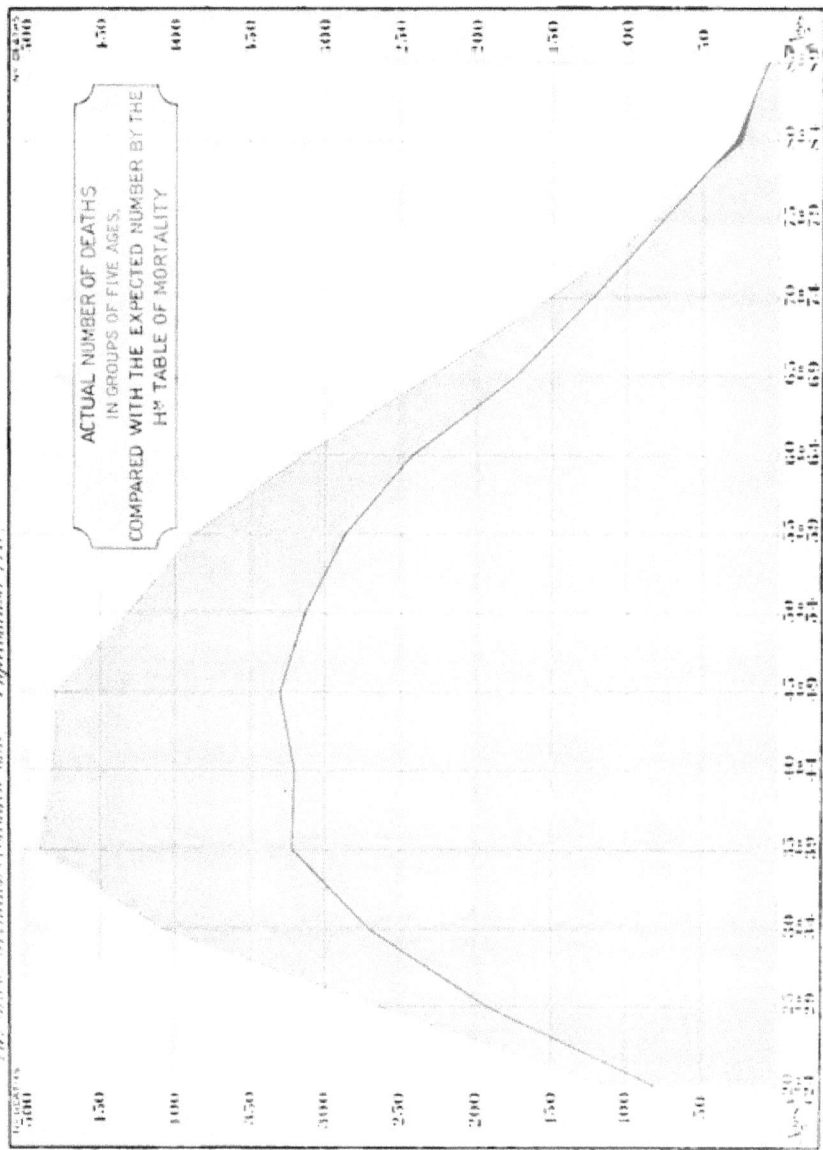

ACTUAL NUMBER OF DEATHS
IN GROUPS OF FIVE AGES,
COMPARED WITH THE EXPECTED NUMBER BY THE
Hᴹ TABLE OF MORTALITY

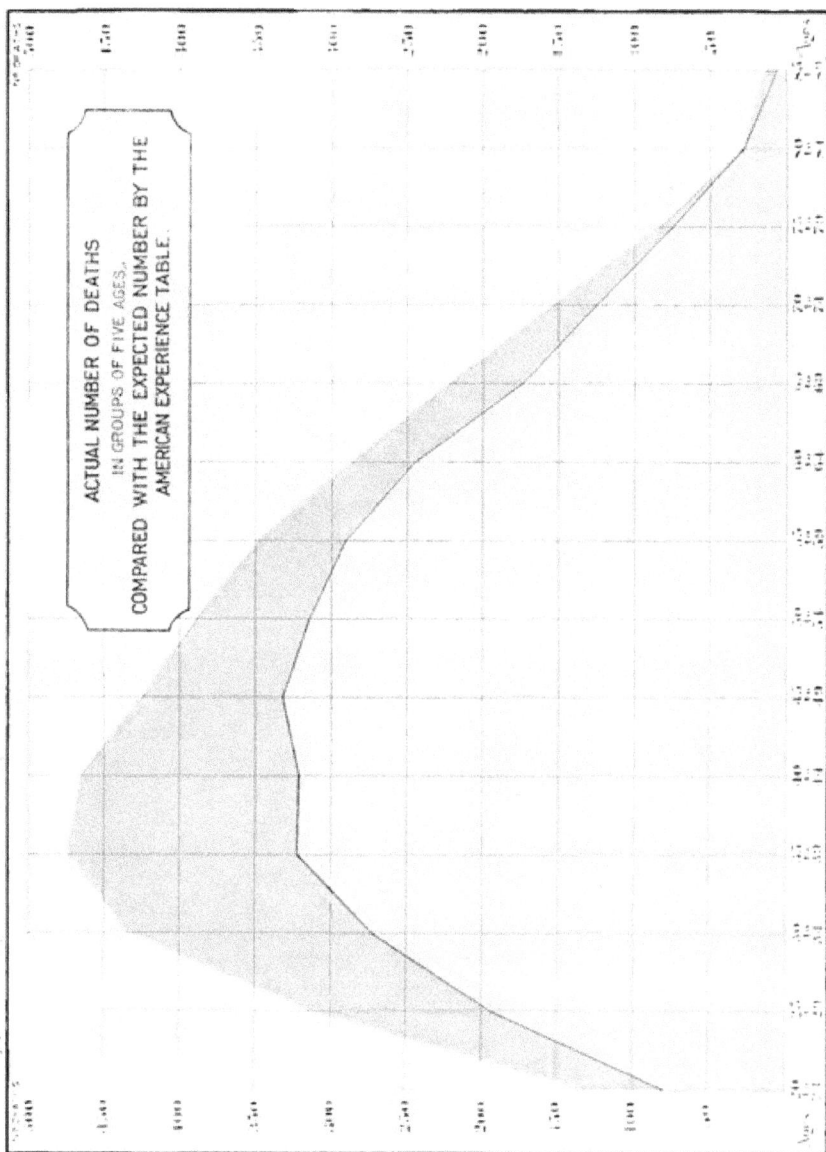

ACTUAL NUMBER OF DEATHS

IN GROUPS OF FIVE AGES,

COMPARED WITH THE EXPECTED NUMBER BY THE
AMERICAN EXPERIENCE TABLE.

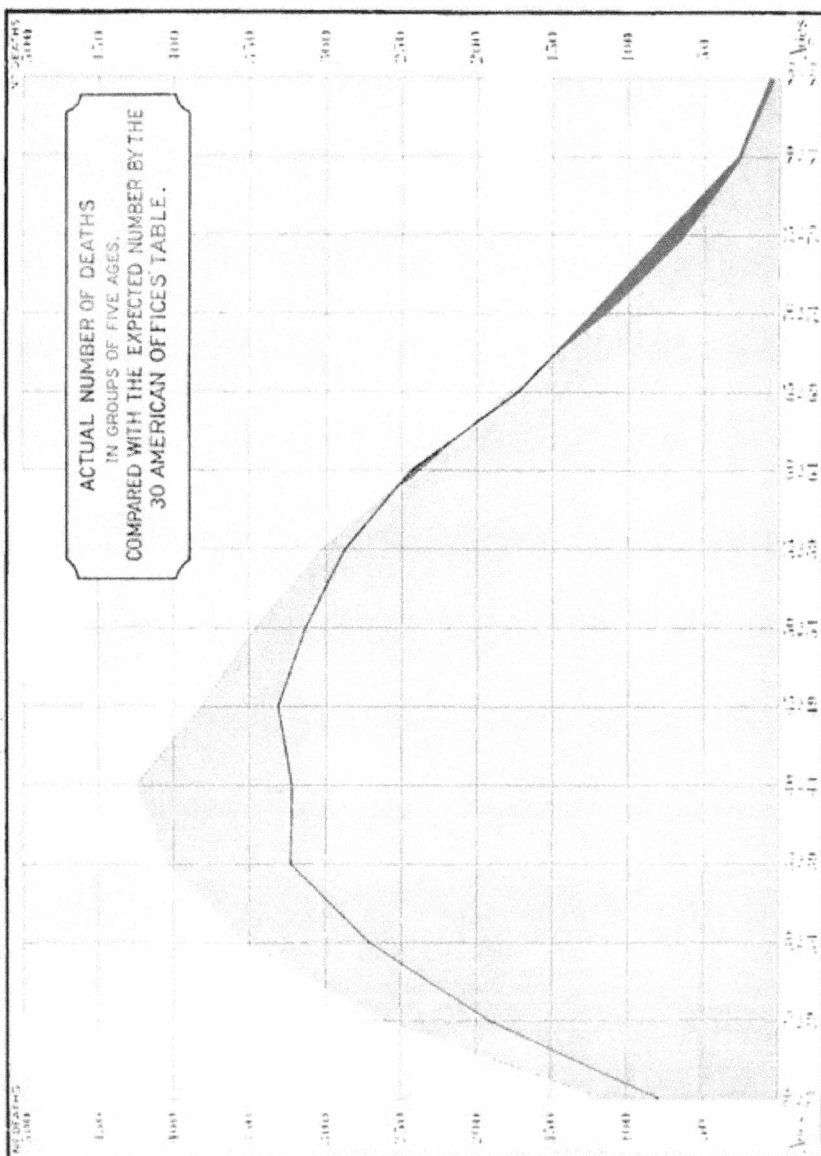

ACTUAL NUMBER OF DEATHS
IN GROUPS OF FIVE AGES,
COMPARED WITH THE EXPECTED NUMBER BY THE
30 AMERICAN OFFICES' TABLE.

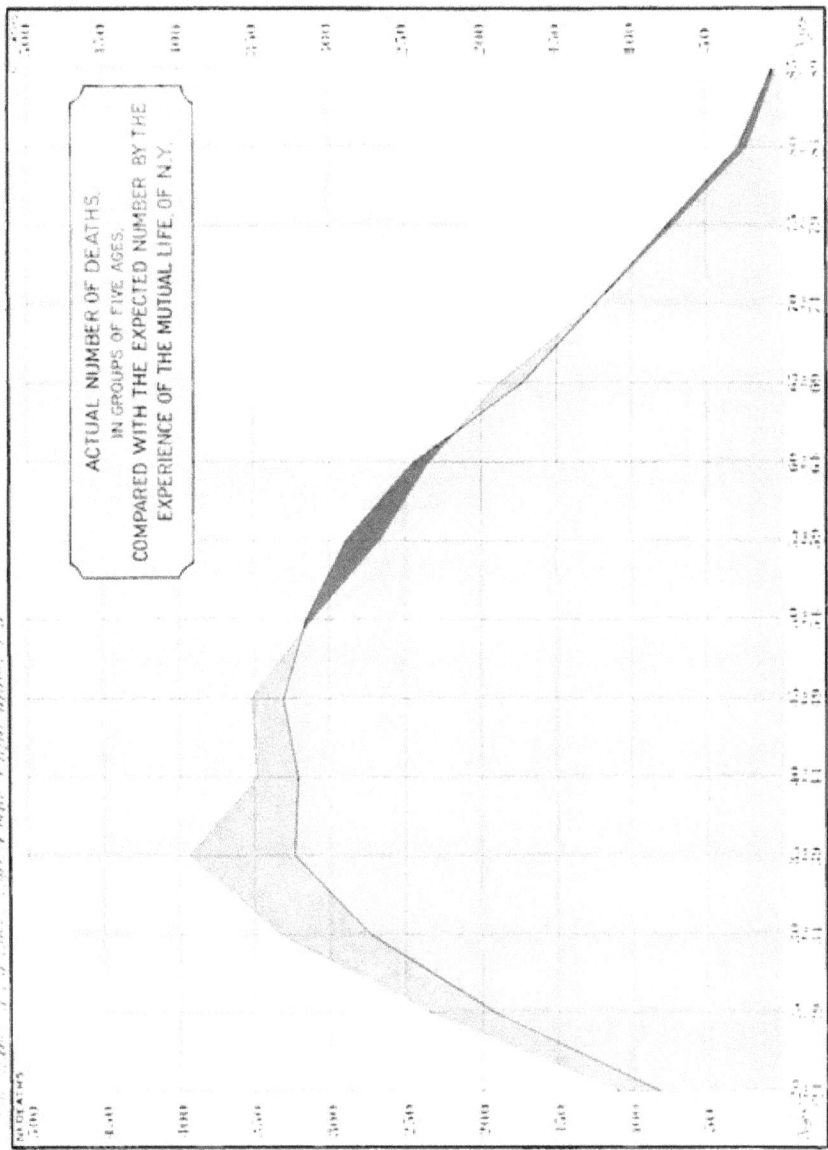

ACTUAL NUMBER OF DEATHS,
IN GROUPS OF FIVE AGES,
COMPARED WITH THE EXPECTED NUMBER BY THE
EXPERIENCE OF THE MUTUAL LIFE OF N.Y.

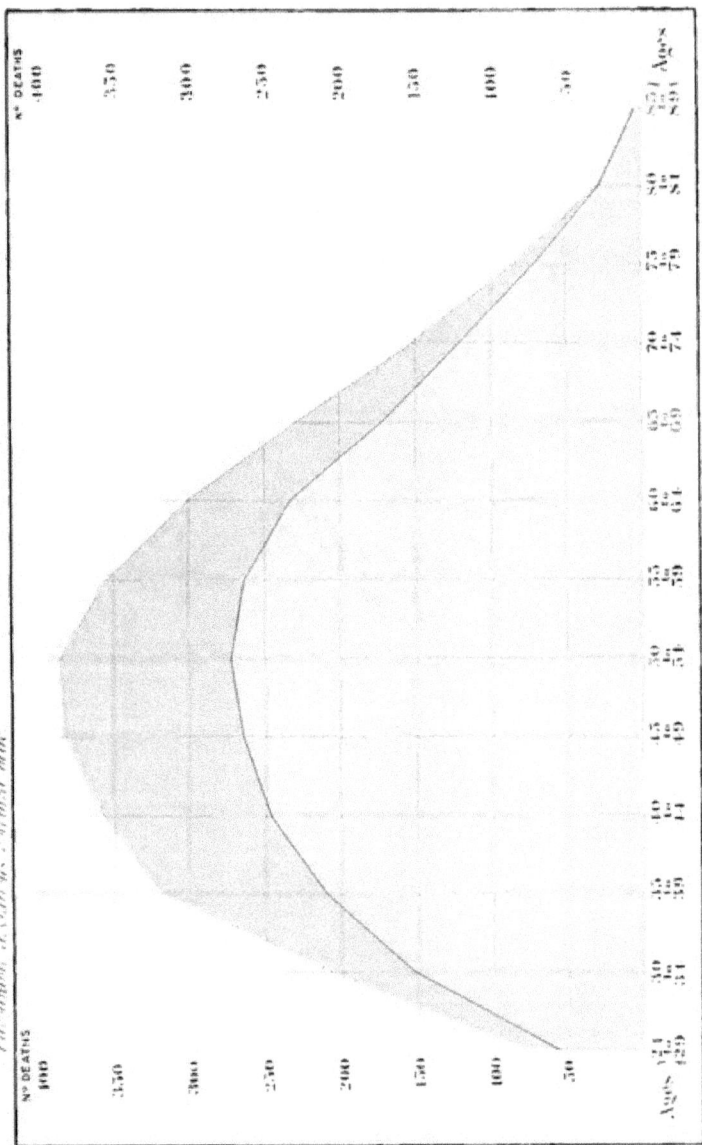

ACTUAL DEATHS IN GROUPS OF FIVE AGES. EXCLUDING FIRST FIVE YEARS OF ASSURANCE.
COMPARED WITH THE EXPECTED NUMBER BY THE INSTITUTE OF ACTUARIES H^M EXPERIENCE.

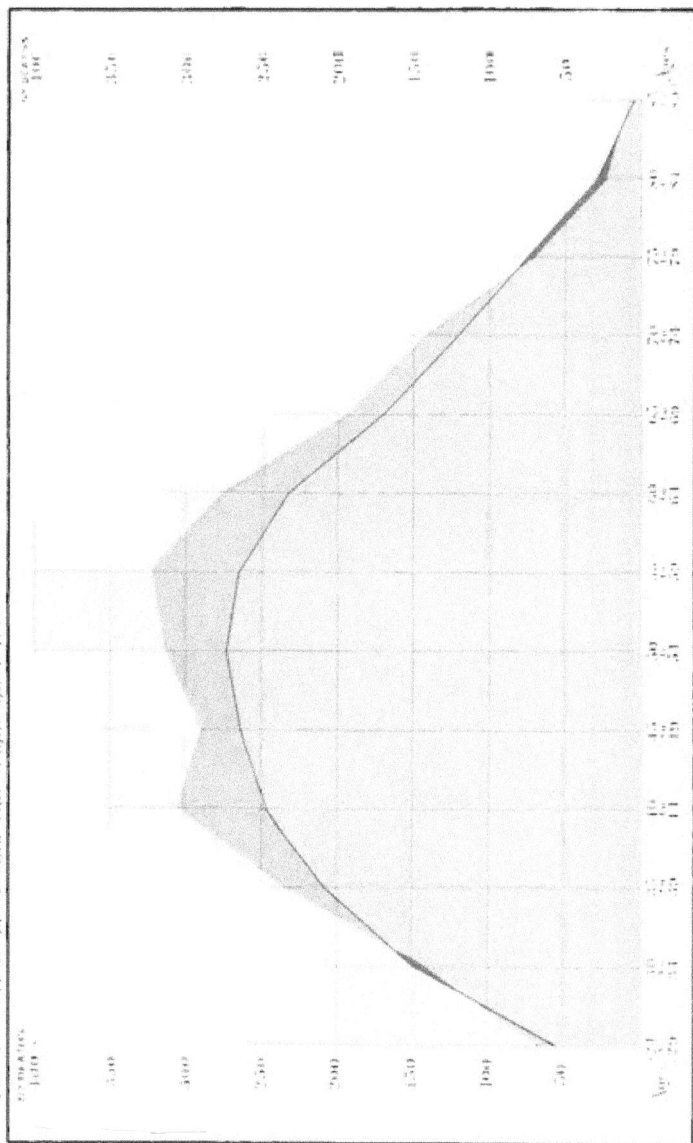

VI

ACTUAL DEATHS IN GROUPS OF FIVE AGES, EXCLUDING THE FIRST FIVE YEARS OF ASSURANCE,
COMPARED WITH THE EXPECTED NUMBER BY THE SCOTTISH WIDOWS FUND EXPERIENCE.

VII

ACTUAL DEATHS IN GROUPS OF FIVE AGES EXCLUDING FIRST FIVE YEARS OF ASSURANCE.
COMPARED WITH THE EXPECTED NUMBER BY THE EXPERIENCE OF THE MUTUAL LIFE OF N.Y.

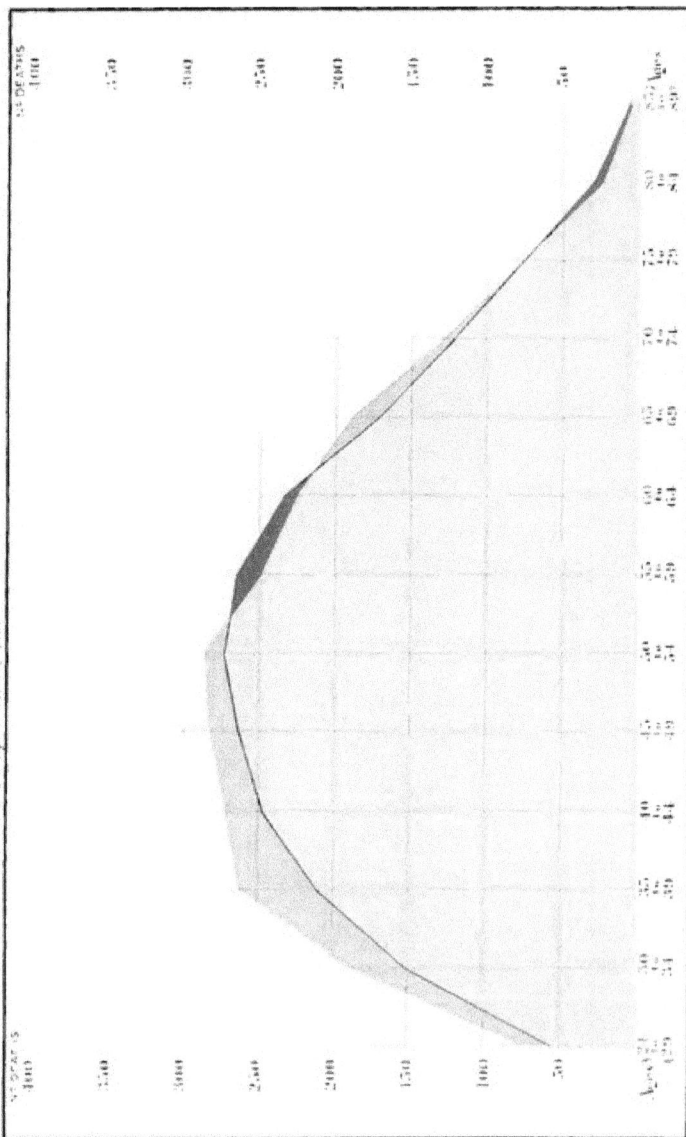

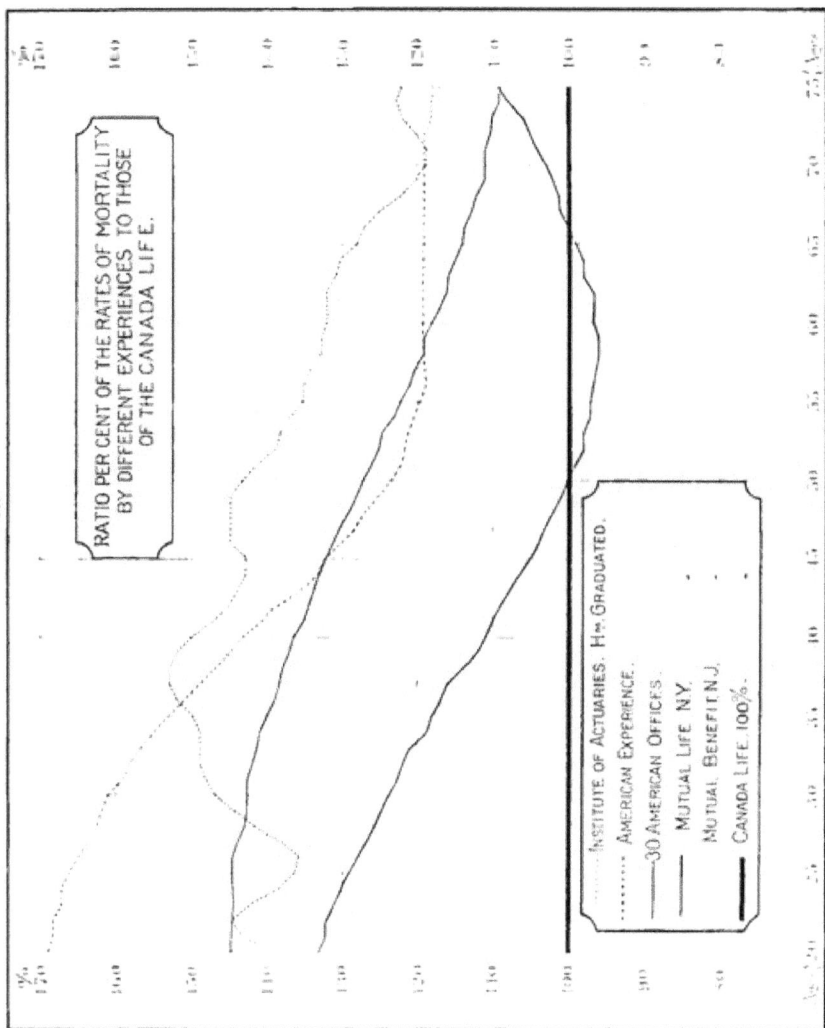

VIII

RATIO PER CENT OF THE RATES OF MORTALITY
BY DIFFERENT EXPERIENCES TO THOSE
OF THE CANADA LIFE.

INSTITUTE OF ACTUARIES. HM GRADUATED.
AMERICAN EXPERIENCE.
30 AMERICAN OFFICES.
MUTUAL LIFE N.Y.   "
MUTUAL BENEFIT N.J.   "
CANADA LIFE 100%.   "

www.ingramcontent.com/pod-product-compliance
Lightning Source LLC
Chambersburg PA
CBHW032245080426
42735CB00008B/1012